SO YOU THINK YOU CAN BE

YOU CAN BE

PRIME

MINISTER

SO YOU THINK YOU CAN BE PRIME MINISTER

IAN MARTIN

Would the country choose YOU?

BLOOMSBURY PUBLISHING

LONDON • OXFORD • NEW YORK • NEW DELHI • SYDNEY

BLOOMSBURY PUBLISHING
Bloomsbury Publishing Plc
50 Bedford Square, London, WC1B 3DP, UK
29 Earlsfort Terrace, Dublin 2, Ireland

BLOOMSBURY, BLOOMSBURY PUBLISHING and the
Diana logo are trademarks of Bloomsbury Publishing Plc

First published in Great Britain 2024
Text copyright © Ian Martin, 2024
Illustrations copyright © Hanna Melin, 2024

A catalogue record for this book is available from
the British Library

ISBN: HB: 978-1-5266-8318-2; eBook: 978-1-5266-8317-5;
ePDF: 978-1-5266-8316-8

2 4 6 8 10 9 7 5 3 1
Typeset by Office of Craig
Printed and bound in Great Britain by CPI Group (UK) Ltd,
Croydon CR0 4YY

To find out more about our authors and books visit
www.bloomsbury.com and sign up for our newsletters

CONTENTS

ACKNOWLEDGEMENTS

Thanks to Eileen Martin for her help with research. Thanks to my agents Abby Singer and CJ Rock from Casarotto Ramsay & Associates, to Grace Paul and Rose Brown from Bloomsbury, and to the magic of serendipity. Chuffed that Hanna Melin agreed to do illustrations – she used to brighten a column I did in the *Architects' Journal* in the late 19th Century. No thanks whatsoever to former prime minister Rishi Sunak, who was supposed to co-ordinate a general election with this book's publication date. And thanks to current prime minister Keir Starmer for being underwhelming enough (so far) to justify the book's title. Lastly, thanks to you – the best prime minister we haven't had.

A NOTE ON THE AUTHOR

Ian Martin is an Emmy award-winning comedy writer and producer. His screen credits include the BAFTA-winning *BBC* series *The Thick of It* (for which he was originally brought in by Armando Iannucci as 'swearing consultant'); BAFTA-nominated *The Death of Stalin* (National Society of Film Critics Award, Best Screenplay); the multi-Emmy award-winning *Veep* (for which he won an Emmy and two Writers' Guild of America awards) and HBO's *Avenue 5*. He also wrote for the Oscar-nominated film In *The Loop*. His comedy-drama *The Hartlepool Spy* won the Tinniswood Award for Best Radio Drama in 2020. From 2000-2005 he edited the cult satirical website *martian.fm*. His previous books include *Epic Space*, *The Coalition Chronicles* and *Lost in the Attic*. He lives in Lancaster, where he runs a primary school writing workshop.

INTRODUCTION

Most of us know our limitations, especially when it comes to a career choice. We watch documentaries about A&E departments and the heroes who work there, and we think no. Oh no, thanks very much. We wouldn't have the nerve, or the stamina, or the resilience to do THAT.

But who among us hasn't looked at the woeful performance of a prime minister and thought: 'Really? Is that all there is to it? Even I could do that.' We watch them on TV, floundering their way through a tough interview, answering questions that weren't asked, ignoring ones that were, trying to brazen it out with a fixed smile. And we think: you know you're lying. The interviewer knows. We know. You must know we all know. But you don't care.

Why on earth would you want to become, sooner or later, the most reviled person in the country? All political careers end in failure, and the bigger they come, the harder they fail. The only dignified exit for a PM seems to be halfway through a term on health grounds. Which isn't a brilliant prospect either, let's face it. Maybe you want to be prime minister because you like bossing people about. Good luck with that, sunshine. The threat of a backbench rebellion, or an exquisitely timed high-profile resignation, can have a faltering PM on the ropes in hours. Good luck, too, throwing your weight around on the international stage. Britain may once have swaggered its way around the globe, but we are in changed circumstances these days. We've left the EU, the Commonwealth is dissolving and the issue of independence for Wales and Scotland isn't going away. You want to be prime minister of... England?

You know best, I suppose. The good news is that it's a *lot* quicker to become prime minister these days. No more lifetime of service in the House of Commons, heaving your way up the party ladder decade by decade. Keir Starmer only entered Parliament in 2015. Didn't take HIM long, did it? It's entirely possible that soon someone could fluke a by-election and then within six years be entertaining half the United Nations in a gazebo in the 10 Downing Street garden.

It's possible, of course, that you want to be prime minister as part of your career trajectory beyond politics, and who can blame you. A few years in the boss's chair does seem to set people up with lucrative political afterlives.

Perhaps you're convinced that you'll find an easier way of doing the job. Again, if the last few years have taught British politicians anything at all it is the staggering potential to skive off the job, to coast through a five-year term in as frictionless way as possible. It's true that there are those politicians who have a reputation for being extremely diligent constituency MPs: putting in the hours, chasing up and badgering various bureaucracies on behalf of those they represent – some of whom may not even have voted for them! Yeah, there are MPs like that. And there are others who find ways to delegate, to fob off, to ignore, while they use their status as a Member of Parliament as an influence lever, finding ways to attract inducements (could be anything, is always money) to say the right thing in select committee meetings or Commons debates.

But perhaps you're being misjudged. Who knows, perhaps you're an innovator, a maverick. You know all the strengths and weaknesses in the system. You want to become an MP and eventually a PM because you know that this creaking institution, crammed into a preposterous disintegrating Gothic horror set, is overdue for reform inside and out. You are a new broom. You aim to bring a new moral astringency to politics, a new transparency and accountability. You have a grand masterplan to move the Houses of Parliament to somewhere more efficient and cost-effective – an architectural marvel further down the Thames, all glass and steel and smart technology – and to convert the current building into some *Harry Potter* Mugglevania hotel and experience centre, or whatever.

Maybe you're just one of those people who believe in democracy, want to make a difference in life, and are keen to pursue a life of service. You want to get the top job not because you're venal and power-mad, but because you are kind-hearted and keen. And you're right, people like you do still exist and the world of politics is always enriched by your being part of it. Your motives are admirable and everyone should applaud you.

Or maybe – and bear with me here – you're an idiot. Perhaps you think you're the only person in the world who can do this job because at school they held pretend elections and you were voted Benign Dictator for Life because of your hilarious manifesto. It promised free ice cream and an end to all homework. You've never forgotten it, have you? And in your head you now think the intervening years were wasted, that your career is taking you nowhere, that you're ready to swing into the 'politics game' the way you swung into IT or the 'catering game'. And that by putting 'game' after politics it shows you already know the rules, that you're a player, that you could take 'that whole being prime minister thing' by the scruff of the neck and turn yourself into the garlanded, globally admired future Nobel Prize winner you know you've always deserved to be.

It wouldn't hurt, though, to familiarise yourself with what the job of prime minister *actually is,* would it? This interactive primer gives you a brief introduction to the craft and mystery of being PM, with little initiative tests to see if you've got what it takes. You'll learn about media schmoozing, donor targeting, campaign organising, how to construct a formidable public persona and so much more.

Whatever your reason for wanting to be prime minister, it's bound to be solid and grounded in logic and reason. And yeah, you know what? You're right. You'd be perfect.

Good luck!

Here's a snap test to see if you have the right general mindset to be PM. Please just answer **YES** or **NO** to each question. You need to get at least half right to be potential PM material.

1. *Are you prepared for political compromise?*

   YES ☆   **NO** ☆

2. *Does standing at a lectern make you feel important?*

   YES ☆   **NO** ☆

3. *Can you look a nation in the eye without blinking?*

   YES ☆   **NO** ☆

4. *Would you dress up as a friendly llama for Red Nose Day?*

   YES ☆   **NO** ☆

5. *Would you allow questions from the press after your inaugural speech?*

   YES ☆   **NO** ☆

6. *Will you tell* OK! Magazine *what your favourite biscuit is?*

   YES ☆   **NO** ☆

7. *Are you 'very, very, very patriotic'?*

   YES ☆   **NO** ☆

8. *Could you, in an emergency, make yourself cry?*

   YES ☆   **NO** ☆

Answers on page 237

Throughout the book you will see PM Q-Cards featuring some past prime ministers. One of these could be your inspiration, your political lighthouse. But who? The scores are entirely subjective – if you don't agree, cross them out and do your own.

Why not imagine yourself as PM and create your own card with some signature policies and massive popularity?

The last Liberal PM. He oversaw the end of World War I, demanding the 'uttermost farthing' from Germans in reparations. The Housing and Town Planning Act built hundreds of thousands of new homes 'fit for heroes' and established the concept of housing as a social service. He also brought about the creation of national insurance and the Irish Free State.

David LLOYD GEORGE
LIBERAL
In office: 1916-1922

Months as PM	71
Largest Commons majority	238
Bullshit rating	7
Chaos factor	4
Legacy impact	7

He was the only PM to have had Welsh as his first language. His popularity tanked with a cash-for-honours scandal, so quite the innovator. He had charged ten grand for a knighthood, which sounds like a bargain, but wasn't. Economic downturn and a wave of strikes ushered him out. He called Hitler the 'greatest living German' and promised World War II wouldn't happen. Had a reputation as a philanderer. Vibe: horny Ewok.

ENJOY
STEADY PAY
EVERY DAY
AS A
P M

"Symbol of Success"

THIS IS THE HOME STUDY COURSE that can change your whole life.

ORDER ONLINE TODAY

NAME

EMAIL

CITY

www.PM.tam

PART ONE

If you're serious about becoming prime minister – of course you are, you're a serious person with noble ambitions – it might help to learn a little about the role itself.

There's not much in the way of a job description available; in the end, most PMs just sort of wing it. But in this section you'll learn a little about the evolution of the post, with a look at how various prime ministers in the past have conducted their days, and a journey through time to see how the gladiatorial spectacle of Prime Minister's Questions has developed, and how this weekly diss battle might evolve to accommodate someone like you in the role. Someone with fresh ideas and a determination to leave their mark. Oh yeah – you'll definitely be a PM to remember.

Here and there are tests and quizzes, offering a simulation of the kind of decisions faced by prime ministers. And a chance to recreate the hostile atmosphere of the House of Commons in your own living room, with Family Christmas PMQs. Practise your political assassination skills on your nearest and dearest, and invite them to do the same. Because politics begins at home...

CHAPTER 1:
A SHORT HISTORY OF THE OFFICE OF PRIME MINISTER

How has the office of prime minister evolved over the three centuries of its existence? It won't surprise you to learn that the bastards *simply made it up as they went along.*

There is no record of the post being brought formally into existence or – according to a parliamentary committee report in 2014 – of any decision to create it. There's no constitutional definition of a PM's role; the Cabinet Manual simply notes that the prime minister is the head of government with 'few statutory functions'.

Yeah, exactly. We're all thinking the same thing. This job is wide open. Maybe it's time for a prime minister to take FULL ADVANTAGE of the sketchy job description. Even Walter Bagehot, the great neurotic constitutional i-dotter and t-crosser, decreed that the monarch heads up the 'dignified' part and the PM leads the 'efficient' bit. *You don't even have to be dignified.* This has been painfully obvious from the reported behaviour inside Number 10 in recent years of course. But it's nice to know that when you make it to the top job you can start living like a hedonistic lottery winner. Suitcases full of booze, all your mates round, Partygate every night, the Cabinet table strewn with lager cans and takeaway cartons, a set of Waterford crystal goblets commemorating the Coronation of His Majesty King Charles the Third crudely repurposed as ashtrays.

It's easy to believe that certain twenty-first century prime minsters have besmirched a role honoured in the past by selfless and patriotic servants of the state. But honestly? The first was the worst.

Dance Around the Walpole

The acknowledged prototype for prime minister, Sir Robert Walpole (1676–1745), was a venal, acquisitive power broker. Wait, this is starting to sound... resonant. He used money and influence to keep himself at the centre of politics for decades, despite being impeached for corruption when leader of the opposition in 1712 and spending months in the Tower of London, where he cultivated his reputation as a Whig martyr. He was First Lord of the Treasury, and prime minister, for 21 years (1721–42). Just imagine the carnage today if someone stayed in power that long.

Popular both within Parliament and outside it – Walpole appealed to centrists 300 years before it became very fashionable – seems to have made him an easy target for satirists. John Gay parodied him as the criminal Jonathan Wild in his *Beggar's Opera.* Walpole's other tormentors included Jonathan Swift, Alexander Pope, Henry Fielding, and Samuel Johnson, which might make him the most celebrity-roasted PM of all time. In today's terms that would be like our current prime minister being mocked by some people off the telly. Still, Walpole bagged that iconic townhouse for the nation: George II liked him enough to present him with 10 Downing Street, which has remained the official PM residence ever since.

The two main political factions then were the Tories (Catholic, monarchist) and the Whigs (anti-Catholic, believed in the supremacy of Parliament). Both derived from derogatory terms: 'whigamores' were anti-Catholic Scottish Presbyterians; 'tories' were Catholic highwaymen and robbers in Ireland. This tradition persists today. Labour are often berated for their humourless moralising, and Tories for their highway robbery.

The phrase 'prime minister' was originally a term of abuse, a suspiciously French expression suggesting that a member of the court had risen above their station ('Attention, you insufferable arriviste! You think you are better than us? I invite you into the coach-park where we may settle this, like fops!'). The idea of a prime minister was thought to be incredibly self-aggrandising, as the monarch was assumed to have all that first-among-equals shit nailed, what with his being sovereign and all.

WORD SEARCH

F	I	L	I	B	U	S	T	E	R	P	Q	Z
L	A	S	G	E	R	H	W	F	K	R	N	B
A	X	Y	C	F	U	X	R	E	D	O	F	N
C	E	A	R	E	C	U	S	A	L	R	L	O
S	Q	F	U	C	I	M	B	Q	V	O	F	I
E	A	E	W	V	N	H	X	E	K	G	Y	T
W	P	A	I	R	I	N	G	C	N	U	P	U
Y	Z	I	U	D	E	X	A	B	O	E	B	L
A	N	X	Q	O	W	S	P	A	D	F	W	O
Y	W	P	C	F	L	T	I	C	K	Y	E	S
D	E	I	B	O	J	S	A	G	P	U	N	S
W	F	H	O	F	N	G	I	E	N	E	F	I
A	I	W	U	D	T	S	Y	X	O	R	P	D

PAIRING ☐   SPAD ☐

PROXY ☐   WHIP ☐

DISSOLUTION ☐   WOOLSACK ☐

RESIGN ☐   PROROGUE ☐

RECUSAL ☐   FILIBUSTER ☐

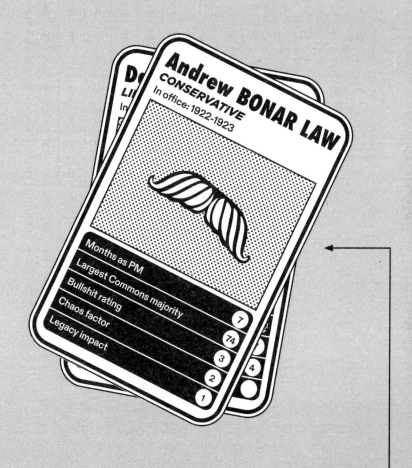

Andrew BONAR LAW

CONSERVATIVE

In office: 1922-1923

Months as PM	7
Largest Commons majority	74
Bullshit rating	3
Chaos factor	2
Legacy impact	1

Shortest-serving PM of the twentieth century. Against Irish home rule. Resigned on health grounds, died six months later, and was the first British PM to be cremated. Vibe: political scorchmark.

Cabinet Making

In the late seventeenth century the powers of Britain's constitutional monarchy were limited, a bit. Then, during the eighteenth century, the Cabinet emerged: first as a theory, then as a convivial gathering of blokes in wigs operating without oversight from the crowned head of state. There was a subtle but telling shift from a monarch ruling through their ministers to a prime minister and colleagues governing 'through the instrumentality of the Crown' – in much the same way as the emerging laws of physics at the time might be said to be operating through the instrumentality of God.

The prime minister is always First Lord of the Treasury too. Walpole was much more comfortable with that title than with the French frippery of PM. But by the time William Pitt the Younger was first minister (among equals) he bloody loved it, and made it clear that there was a genuine need for 'an avowed and real Minister, possessing the chief weight in the Council and the principal place in the confidence of the King' and started using the term freely, as did *The Times,* which, by 1805, was using 'prime minister' in reports of parliamentary debates.

Gradually, Then Suddenly

Some people are never satisfied, though. Or are they? In 1878, William Gladstone (prime minister four times in the nineteenth century) said that nowhere in the world 'was there a man who has so much power, with so little to show for it in the way of formal title or prerogative', which sounds like he's moaning at not being able to publicly execute his enemies in Trafalgar Square, when he's actually hinting that he can do more than you might ever imagine, mate, so don't push your fucking luck.

Historian Lord Blake identified three turning points in the development of the prime minister's role:

★ 1782–4: Switch from the monarch being head of the executive and actively concerned with government, to a monarch with the power of veto: to dismiss a PM on the grounds that he didn't much like the cut of his jib, or indeed his policies.

★ 1834–5: Shift from 'king's government' to party government.

★ 1867–84: Move from government by parties based in Parliament to government by parties based on nationwide organisations.

To which perhaps we shall have to add:

★ 2038–45: Massive honking swerve from existing powers of the prime minister to a totally new set of rules brutally forced through Parliament by a new, iconoclastic PM. You.

Make the Job Your Own

... and own the job you make. Scenario: you are now prime minister. You are allowed one major amendment to the powers vested in you by the office. What's it to be? Will you be giving yourself more power over...

The king? It's high time the monarchy knew its place in the twenty-first century. State ceremonies in fancy dress, opening new wildlife reserves, waving, smiling and doing their little posho videos: yes. Interfering at any level with your government: no. From now on the king comes to you for briefings. All pretence that he's anything other than a lucky DNA-inheritor, rather than a notional head of state: gone. Your new powers mean you don't need any permission to prorogue Parliament, or anything else. You could even start calling it the Prime Minister's Speech, and sit on the throne in the crazy royal outfit yourself, why not? (For an alternative relationship with the king, see **A Very British COO**, page 202.)

The church? Time to separate church and state properly. Make the Archbishop of Canterbury a civil service job with sensible clothes and full accountability. Also, let's get rid of the bishops in the House of Lords – we're not a theocracy. Give yourself the power of veto over any Christmas or Easter address by anyone in the church, make sure they all keep things nice and apolitical.

The Lords? Yes, never mind the bishops, give yourself the power to abolish hereditary peers. People should not be able to interfere with the law-making process just because their dad owned half of Dorset and had a lifetime season ticket to the House of Lords. If anyone wants a seat in the Lords they should pay the going rate to your party's treasurer.

The opposition? Gone are the days of MPs being sent to the Tower to 'purge their contempt', and more's the pity. Give yourself powers to properly bring back some much-needed discipline to the Commons. Restore the ancient tradition (which you've just unearthed) of arming the Speaker, who will be allowed to shoot anyone for un-parliamentary behaviour, such as being overly sarcastic at PMQs. Have bailiffs dressed in Tudor armour on hand to physically remove dissenters and irritating types. And watch the viewing figures for *BBC Parliament* soar. Maybe even have ad breaks.

Your own party? There have been some disturbing scenes in the Commons in recent years. Scuffles in the voting lobbies. Flagrant defiance of the party line by maverick MPs. A united party means a strong government. 'Withdrawing the whip' may not be much of a threat, but 'using the whip' might. What's the point of having party whips if they haven't even got actual whips? Or at the very least, big truncheons. Give yourself the power of violence over your MPs, free from the risk of any legal consequences, and feel the party loyalty swell!

TRUE OR FALSE?

1. As part of psychological preparations for his second term, Tony Blair employed a hypnotherapist who taught him how to see the world from a height of 2.5 metres.

TRUE ☆   **FALSE** ☆

2. Theresa May's favourite Beano character was Minnie the Minx.

TRUE ☆   **FALSE** ☆

3. During his school holidays Rishi Sunak worked as a waiter in a Southampton curry house.

TRUE ☆   **FALSE** ☆

4. David Lloyd George was a skilled ventriloquist and once made a basket of eggs address his mistress Frances Stevenson in a variety of Welsh voices.

TRUE ☆   **FALSE** ☆

5. After the Daily Mirror ran a headline - 'Fat prime minister Gordon should lose weight, says diet expert' - Brown switched from 4 Kit-Kats a day to 9 bananas.

TRUE ☆   **FALSE** ☆

6. Margaret Thatcher slept for only four hours a night, bolt upright, with her eyes open, in a velvet padded coffin, reciting the Bible.

TRUE ☆   **FALSE** ☆

7. James Callaghan and his wife Audrey owned three Yorkshire Terriers called Bonny, Scamp and Twerp.

TRUE ☆   FALSE ☆

8. John Major had a two-year affair with a Downing Street caterer.

TRUE ☆   FALSE ☆

9. Stanley Baldwin was a cousin of Horatio Kipling, the master baker after whom Mr Kipling cakes were named.

TRUE ☆   FALSE ☆

10. Anthony Eden swam the Channel as a young man, twice - once from England to France and once from France to England.

TRUE ☆   FALSE ☆

Answers on page 238

CHAPTER 2:
WHAT DOES A PM *DO*?

What do you think they do? Wrong. When you think they're busy, they're napping. When you think they're on downtime at Chequers, the prime ministerial retreat, they're in panicky meetings with special advisers until the early hours. Can you nap? AND panic? Maybe you could be PM!

Every Wednesday there's a first, friendly question lobbed to the PM at Prime Minister's Question Time. It asks the PM what they've been up to today: 'Mr Speaker, this morning I had meetings with ministerial colleagues and others...' But did they? Meetings about what?

Cabinet meetings, for instance, have been very different in tone from era to era. The Churchill-led coalition government of 1940–45 saw pipe and cigarette smoke hanging like smog in the air, awful catering, compulsory prayers, singing all the verses of the national anthem accompanied by the Royal Harmonica Player, casual Freemasonry, no women or minorities, and vicious factional in-fighting.

What a contrast to the Blair administration of 1997–2007, which saw no smoking, an extended moment of religious or secular personal reflection, fruit and pastries, several Mexican waves around the Cabinet table to communal shouts of 'Yay! Whatever works!', inclusivity, inclusivity, inclusivity, and vicious factional in-fighting.

Dear Diary...

The difference between Churchill and Blair is even more striking when we look at their personal diaries. These give us fascinating insights into their contrasting styles of government.

Churchill's peace

Here's Churchill recording a day's events in April 1953, by which point his time as an international statesman were well behind him.

9 a.m. *woke with filthy hangover, set aside further hour of 'thinking time' in bed.*

10 a.m. ~~*woken again*~~ *v important paperwork interrupted by Mrs Grenville-Withers with my breakfast: grouse baked in its own blood, 1 doz. potato cakes, 3 hard-boiled eggs, swan giblets, tinned grapefruit, wherewithal for several large scotches & soda, black pills, pink pills, half-doz. cigars, 1lb. Everton Mints.*

Noon: *working bath with War Cabinet. Much easier now bathroom extended to accommodate raked seating. V convenient, nobody can hear you p*ss or spill your brandy. V disappointed with war situation i.e. no decent bloody wars any more, grr. Half-arsed Korean affair winding down, Stalin on last legs, who the blazes are we supposed to be at war with, eh? Asked Gen. Law to see if he couldn't destabilise the Balkans for a few months. Need war as much as I need air to breathe or alcohol to drink. War. WAR! 1 jug gin and tonic, 2 dozen sausages.*

1 p.m. *downstairs in jimjams to sign correspondence, conferred with ministers, 1 bottle champagne, 2 doz. oysters, wrote speech for Commons later.*

2 p.m. *nap.*

3 p.m. *stayed in bed for Cabinet meeting. Discussed plans for the Coronation of our beautiful new Queen. Also bloody silly No-More Rationing Knees-Ups: ugh, ghastly street parties, smog, Belisha Beacons, trade unions, Communists. 1 bot. Riesling, half-doz. sherries (3 sweet, 3 dry), sauteed pig's balls.*

4 p.m. *nap.*

6 p.m. *read papers, dictated letters, had another bath, got dressed.*

7 p.m. *thinking nap.*

8 p.m. *dinner. 2 bots. champagne, black pudding, haggis and scallops, suckling pig, roast potatoes, boiled potatoes, mashed potatoes and chips. And a baked potato. 1 bot. Viognier, 1 bot. claret. 16 choc. eclairs, Battenburg cake, 4 large Armagnacs, two cigars at once, big coffee.*

9 p.m. *Address House of C on subject of future wars, how an Iron Curtain is descending upon Europe, how we must stand with the Eastern States against the Russian Bear, the modest integrity of the British People and the importance of revering national heroes. Enormous waves of hear-hears and rustlings of papers in acclamation. Up to Members Dining Room for light supper. 2 quail, 1 doz. lamb chops, 5 bots. champagne in company of amusing sycophants and dear friends.*

11 p.m. *back in jimjams, chaired committee meetings until 2 a.m. in bed. Absinthe, medicinal cigarettes, hookah pipe, several white ports.*

3 a.m. *doctor attended for indigestion, administered sleeping aid.*

The Care Blairs

By the time Tony Blair swept to power on a tide of exhaustion with John Major's government, things were very different. It was the late 1990s: a time of hope. The job of prime minister was seen as more presidential and metropolitan. Less alcoholic, more workaholic. At about the time Churchill was going to sleep, Blair was just getting up, as this May 1998 diary entry reveals.

3 a.m. *Both an unholy start to the day, and a holy one! I wake up and make my way to the old Number 10 game pantry, a rather bleak space unused since the days of Churchill, when various species of blameless slaughtered birds would be hung until they were utterly disgusting. Geruesome. Thank God, I say, for the abolition of both hanging and game pantries! These days it's a calming spiritual space, as Cherie and her feng-shui lifestyle architect, Pippa, have had it converted into a dinky, and very cosy, little Catholic church.*

After some preparatory lunges and a (much-needed!) cappuccino I rendezvous in what we're (ha ha) now calling Quail Mary's with Cherie and Father Donegan for Matins. Nothing fancy – a few Psalms, a chapter of Scripture, some respectful, mumbled prayers – while the rest of the world slumbers on. 'It don't 'alf buck you up, innit!' as kids like us in our forties say these days. Look, seriously, I'm increasingly drawn to Catholicism now the economy is recovering from eighteen years of Tory misrule. Having a direct line to God is going to make it so much easier to avoid the moral perils of my predecessors, e.g. getting drawn into bloodshed on foreign soil just because America feels the need to teach the world a lesson. Cup of tea, cheeky digestive biscuit and back to bed for a bit.

5 a.m. *Briefing at the kitchen table with Tom, Toby, Sophie, Jo, Will and Biz, my special advisers. We discuss this week's Cool Britannia reception at Number 10: nibbles and Cava and mingling with other young people. I'm mad for it! The guest list is brilliant. The acceptable brother from Oasis, Damien Hirst (the half-shark guy), several pairs of fashionable lesbians, that footballer I did the keepy-uppy photoshoot with – Bazza? Gobbo? – Nigella, Swampy, Kate Moss, Sporty Spice, the cast of Trainspotting, the list is endless but can't remember who else. Also discussed: strategy to deal with the looming Millennium Bug chaos, shortlist of personal skateboard tutors, the Pound.*

7 a.m. *Meet Gordon [Brown, Chancellor] in Cabinet Room for economic briefing. We sit at opposite ends of the massive table. As scratchy and competitive as ever, he tells me he's ended 'boom and bust' for ever. I say 'oh, that's good,' he says 'yes, it IS actually,' I say 'I said it was,' he says 'I know it is.' This goes on for twenty-five minutes, then five minutes of silence. We hear Big Ben strike the half-hour, and he leaves without saying a word.*

7.30 a.m. *Ambling back to the old PM pad, listening to Simply Red on my Walkman, when I get the fright of my life. Charging round the corner, coming straight at me in full boxing gear is Alastair Campbell, my press secretary. A punch, right in the midriff! He's shouting at me, as usual. 'ALWAYS!' Punch. 'BE!' Punch. 'FUCKING!' Punch. 'READY!' I point out, breathlessly, that readiness for* *being ambushed and assaulted by my own fucking Head of Narrative seemed until now a pointless exercise. 'Yeah? Remember that, the next time one of your loony-left backbenchers tries it on at Conference,' he mutters, as he skips off down the corridor.*

8 a.m. *Breakfast with Cherie, the children, and a couple of junior breakfast advisers. I value family time and today is no exception. Toast, maybe some porridge (hand-milled oats!) a cursory sneer at the newspapers and a catch-up with The Care Blairs (family). None the wiser, to be honest. All the children want to talk about is 'mobile telephones' and 'the internet'. As if either have any meaningful impact on ordinary people's lives!*

9 a.m. *Horrible interview with the BBC, who, in accordance with their charter, I suppose, are being as cynical as possible about Labour's achievements so far. Some smarmy git called Nick was really insolent, actually: 'Mr Blair, you honestly think that Sure Start Centres, a national minimum wage, record investment in education and the NHS, a rise in child benefit payments, two million people lifted out of poverty, the Good Friday Agreement taking shape and the normalisation of civil partnerships is really enough to convince the electorate that your administration is going to get things done?' Arsehole. Why can't people simply enjoy our New Labour Reality? Things will only keep getting better. No more economic uncertainty. No more wars. Chill out, BBC!*

In the Big Dog House

Not all diaries are so poignant, so heavy with dramatic irony. Although it has to be said: actually, they are. All of them. Fast-forward to February 2020. The prime minister of the day, Boris Johnson, didn't keep a diary on the grounds that he 'couldn't be arsed'. A record of his time in office was assiduously maintained for a while by his diligent and loyal Keeper of the Journal, then a keen and attractive twenty-year-old intern, now Lady Hunterdon of Haggerston, with a life peerage and a lucrative government contract to supply unspecified items of 'IT support'.

9 a.m. *Still no sign of Big Dog (BD). Media and comms teams going tonto. Rumours pinging around Twitter that the PM's already missed heaps of emergency meetings about the Wu Tang Flu, as he hilariously calls it in private. Where IS he? Try Find My Phone. Find the phone: upstairs in child's bedroom still playing a David Walliams audiobook anthology. Oh yes, that's right, says Carrie, he was putting Beowulf to bed last night, wasn't he? Snuck out again, I bet, the shithead. Check the logs: ministerial car probs picked him up. Sure enough, 'Mr Sexwolf, Secretary of State for Bants', taken to Heathrow at about 8.30 p.m. Whereabouts unknown. How am I supposed to write his diary if I don't know what the eff he's doing?*

10 a.m. *Ah, a picture has surfaced of BD in a security queue at a provincial Italian airport. Looks terrible. Totes dishevs, tie all wonky, rumpled face and matching jacket. I think he would have got away with it had it not been for the large plastic tits attached to his chest. BD oblivs, ofc.*

2 p.m. *BD back and very much in the big doghouse, a load of his clothes just dumped on a landing upstairs. Obvs I need to be briefed as must fill in events of last night. Stag do apaz, with some old Bullingdon chums at a place owned by 'mate of a mate, put us all on the VIP list. People kept calling him Comrade, possibly Russian? Just put Messy Night at Villa Bunga-Bunga'. Jesus, bring me a coffee I implore you, and I'll sort you an OBE, I promise.'*

5 p.m. *Despite strict instructions not to be woken until six, BD roused on the urgent demands of the Chief Medical Officer (CMO). Imperative we formulate a plan NOW to deal with the coronavirus, there are serious cases confirmed in London already, blah blah. 100% human buzzkill. BD meanwhile XXL Grumpy at being disturbed, tells CMO it's just bloody flu. Brits can just, er, er, biff it on the nose, let's get on with our lives. CMO says it's ravaging Italian hospitals already, and it'll do same to our dear old lovely NHS. BD has lightbulb – yes, yes! Exactly! Just got back from Italian fact-finder actually, stand down, people over there going bonkers, partying all night, in out, in out, shake it all about... nothing to worry about at all. CMO says that this is serious, Prime Minister. We need to consider lockdown. BD replies that's quite frankly very un-British, and an overreaction.*

6 p.m. *Phew. Things a little calmer now Old Lockdown Moany Med-Head's evaporated, threatening to go straight to the papers with his paranoid ramblings about aerosol transmissions and social distancing. BD, in a really quite sulky countermove, is at St Thomas' Hospital, and I quote: 'shaking every hand I can find – bring out your plague-ridden zombies, I'll roger them all if that's what it takes to show the bloody Medical Stasi that flu isn't dangerous just because it's fucking Chinese!'*

How's Your Day Looking?

The lesson to be gleaned from the three extracts above is that individuals can make the job of prime minister very much their own. So... what sort of PM would you be, do you think? Where would you be on the axis between Power-Hungry Selfish Bastard and Dedicated Public Servant? I mean, you must know yourself, but let's find out, shall we? Please take this multiple-choice quiz and circle your answer. And answer honestly – nobody's looking. Are they?

5.45 a.m. SCENARIO ONE

The start of your day. Number 10 is already busy downstairs. You arrive at the kitchen table, where an aide has left a delicious coffee, or tea if you prefer. Or Bloody Mary, who gives a shit, you're the goddam PRIME MINISTER. Staff are under strict instructions not to disturb you. So. Hmm. There you are, with forty-five minutes to yourself. There's a skip-load of paperwork waiting for you in the official Red Box. On the other hand, there's a new game to play on your personal console, and why not? *You deserve this.* The game developers are very excited to get your read on it. It's good to decompress this early in the day, and there's a ton of balls waiting for you later. What's it to be?

★   Red Box
★   X Box
★   Neither – have a little nap
★   Bit of both: you're all about compromise

8 a.m. SCENARIO TWO

A gaggle of wonks and advisers wait for you in your office. Half an hour this morning has been put aside to approve a draft policy on localised planning permission for new housing in potential floodplain areas. Of course, it's very important. But boring. A PM shouldn't have to deal with this crap. And you've been so busy upstairs you haven't even had breakfast yet. Do you:

★ Push on with the meeting and get breakfast sent in for everyone (even wonks have to eat): this is real front-line stuff.
★ Send an aide in with your apologies, urgent NATO thing, slip back into the kitchen and have a leisurely breakfast.
★ Play NATO card, say you want a formulated draft policy on your desk in one hour you pathetic bumbling wonkfucks, then leave them to it, have a bath AND breakfast.
★ Enter meeting, apologise for a hard out in twenty minutes (NATO business), let's thrash through main points then have a follow-up Zoom to finesse ideas next week.

10 a.m. SCENARIO THREE

You're (happy to help, nothing to hide) appearing before a select committee looking into an alleged culture of bullying at Number 10. One committee member asks you directly if you're aware of the allegations, some of which are about you. Say:

★ 'I am NOT personally aware of any bullying, which of course is something I DEPLORE. And if my behaviour at any time has made anyone feel uncomfortable, I sincerely apologise...'
★ 'We have a robust anti-bullying system in place, like

those train security announcements: See Bullying, Say Bullying, Bullying Sorted. I think if any bullying was occurring, I'd be the first to know, I am after all the bloody PRIME MINISTER.'

★ 'Look, you've worked with fucking interns, you know what they're like. Need a slap and a shake just to activate them, otherwise they're in standby mode all day, the lazy shitheads.'

★ 'If dragging a dedicated servant of the state before a hostile and aggressive committee isn't structured bullying, I don't know what is. Just leave me alone, you sadists!'

12 p.m. SCENARIO FOUR

Cabinet meeting. It's all smiles for five minutes because ITV's getting general coverage for a report on your important new crackdown on whatever it is. Then ITV leaves and the atmosphere plunges. It's clear that your home secretary (Liz) is gathering a little cabal around her, possibly with a view to launching a leadership bid. You need to assert your dominance over these treacherous bastards, right now. What do you do?

★ Draw their attention to the apparently blank sheets of paper being handed out. Announce that you're all going to team-bond with a game of Wink Murder. Everyone turns over their sheet of paper to find out if they're the murderer. They're not. It's you, obviously. Silently dare them to make eye contact, then do them in. Metaphorically. For now.

★ Invite Liz to tell everyone what her thoughts are on loyalty as a government's secret weapon. While she's spluttering nonsense, walk around the table behind them all, in a sinister way. Perhaps every now and then randomly lay a hand on someone's shoulder. But not Liz's.

★ Insist on everyone raising their glasses in a toast to victory. Everyone has a glass. It's just water. Yeah, water that's been POISONED. Oh look, you have the antidote. Who's prepared to swear allegiance NOW?

★ Say you're thinking about having a snap reshuffle. Is there any job in particular they have their eyes on? Liz? Happy at the home office? Or would you like something LESS FUCKING STRESSFUL? Then flip a hand grenade onto the table.

4 p.m. SCENARIO FIVE

An unexpected call from the President of the United States. Heads up: he's authorising a drone strike on a certain Middle East country which is at odds with another Middle East country, an ally. And he wants explicit support from Britain. Awkward. You've just promised the Commons that any military involvement will require the consent of Parliament. But the president wants a decision now: is Britain in, or not? What do you tell him?

★ You're not going to be bounced into another pointless war until you've done a snap public opinion poll. Ask France or someone.

★ Okay, the British army is in, but they'll just do the catering.

★ Say 'Give me 24 hours!' but in a gruff, generic American accent.

★ Tell him this call is terminated, then block him on Facebook.

Answers on page 239

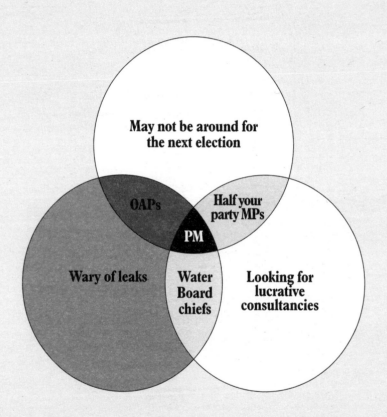

May not be around for the next election

OAPs

Half your party MPs

PM

Wary of leaks

Water Board chiefs

Looking for lucrative consultancies

Helped found Labour and was the first working-class PM. Handsome, a great orator, iconic Labour leader. Extended national insurance benefits and expanded municipal housebuilding. Censured by Conservatives in his first term for not prosecuting the Communist newspaper *Workers' Weekly* (they incited servicemen to mutiny), the Liberals piled on, and Parliament was dissolved.

James RAMSAY MACDONALD
LABOUR
In office: 1929-1935

THE Workers' ⓐ Weekly
Workers of the World Unite!

Months as PM	81
Largest Commons majority	492
Bullshit rating	5
Chaos factor	6
Legacy impact	4

Denounced as traitor by the Labour movement in his second term for forming a National Government (all-party coalition) during Depression years. Expelled from the party. Mental decline towards the end, made less and less sense in the Commons; and in those days people noticed. Vibe: edgy hypnotist.

PM POP QUIZ

1. Which PM developed a tolerance for, and dependence on, stimulants? Their drug regime included benzedrine, barbiturates (sodium amytal and secobarbital), dextroamphetamine, pethidine and promezine.

    A. Liz Truss   **C. Anthony Eden**
    B. Neville Chamberlain   **D. Gordon Brown**

2. Which PM answered the door to find two left-wing students from the University of Aberdeen, who said they were there to kidnap him. To which he replied 'I suppose you realise that if you do, the Conservatives will win the election by 200 or 300...'

    A. John Major   **C. Stanley Baldwin**
    B. Alec Douglas-Home   **D. David Cameron**

3. Who said: 'Without democracy, governments will become corrupt. They will be run by an elite who will hand power to other members of that elite...'

    A. Ramsay MacDonald   **C. Tony Blair**
    B. David Lloyd George   **D. Boris Johnson**

4. Which PM spent a lot of time during a visit to the White House entirely naked in their room?

    A. Margaret Thatcher   **C. Winston Churchill**
    B. Tony Blair   **D. John Major**

5. Who said: 'I have been around this racetrack so often that I cannot generate any more enthusiasm for jumping any more hurdles...'

    A. Harold Wilson   **C. Gordon Brown**
    B. Winston Churchill   **D. Tony Blair**

Answers on page 239

CHAPTER 3:
PRIME MINISTER'S QUESTION TIME

One aspect of prime ministerial life that has definitely coarsened over the years is Prime Minister's Question Time (PMQs). This happens every Wednesday lunchtime and is a sort of tribal pantomime for adults.

Notionally in charge of proceedings is the Speaker, whose job it is to maintain order. In theory, he or she 'directs' the House of Commons. In practice, they sit in a big chair trying to impose their authority in much the same way as a supply teacher supervises a class in detention: MPs idly check their mobile phones, mutter among themselves, occasionally passing notes to one another and sniggering. Whoever is officially talking gets loud approval from their side and jeering noises from the other side.

To the right of the Speaker are the government benches. The prime minister and Cabinet members sit on the front bench. Those MPs representing the governing party sit behind the front bench and are called, rather predictably, backbenchers. To the left of the Speaker are the opposition benches containing their enemies. By convention, backbenchers commend a front bench MP by saying 'hear, hear', which is parliamentary shorthand for 'hear, attend to these most sensible words being expressed most elegantly by my honourable Friend, also let my honourable Friend notice me and the way I am audibly sucking up in the hope of a ministerial post.' These days 'hear hear' is more commonly expressed as a very long noise containing very few consonants, for example 'eeeeayuhaayeeaah.'

PMQs are an opportunity for the prime minister to set out the party's policy programme, but more importantly to trade insults with the opposition. These are routinely 'humorous', although protocol requires that all jokes are written not by professionals but by their socially awkward special advisers, or SPADs. This guarantees that the jokes are mostly shit, but it doesn't matter because the relevant backbenchers make an appreciative noise anyway.

Would you be any good at PMQs? Prime ministers have to be able to think on their feet AND read carefully prepared jokes. Here are official accounts from the early nineteenth century, the twentieth century and the twenty-first century. See for yourself how unsophisticated and bad-tempered this sorry spectacle has become over time.

The fourth PMQs is set in the near future, when you are prime minister. As you'll see, the spots for your magisterial oratory have been left blank. Practice makes perfect. When you've honed your witty responses to perfection, fill in the blanks and see how impressive you sound – probably.

Then, you and some suitable companions are invited to play FAMILY CHRISTMAS PMQs! All you need is this book, a pair of dice and a willingness to fall out, with full recriminations and loaded silences, with your nearest and dearest.

FROM THE ARCHIVES: 1821

The following extract comes from a time when democracy remained securely in the hands of the landed gentry.

The House of Commons

Upon Thursday the 30th day of April in the Year of Our Lord Eighteen Hundred One & Twenty, this being the Feast Day of the Circumcision of St. Paul

Prayers, the Casting Out of Demons, the Chanting of Psalms

The Prime Minister, his Most Urgent Matters, to wit, The Macadamisation of the King's Highways and The Evil Tyranny of Ardent Spirits

---

The Chamber being assembled, the Great Door locked by the Bailiff of the House. Then, three loud Knocks upon the Door.

Chieftain of Pursuivants d'Azure et d'Or, Keeper of Ye Glyphs and Master of Ye King's Pasquinades: Ahoy hoy there! Pip pip, and may all our friends prosper!

The Bailiff: Pip pip! Aye, God save the King and a curse upon all our foes! Who goes there?

Chieftain of Pursuivants: If it please the House I do present the Prime Minister. With snuff and rum for all!

The Bailiff *[unlocking ye Great Door]*: Aye, so say we all! In the Name of God Almighty, I command thee – cause the Prime Minister to Occur!

[The prime minister (the Earl of Liverpool) then entering and most graciously distributing snuff, rum, sundry emoluments and bribes, some hon. Members being already merry from the imbibing of ale and ardent spirits. The prime minister then proposing a toast.]

The Prime Minister: To the King! And to his most loyal Government!

Hon. Members: *cheering, hiccupping, mutterings, intestinal plosions.*

Lord Cornwall of Cornwall: Sir, in rising to call the attention of the House to the Motion of which I have given notice, for a Select Committee to inquire into the dangers of macadamising the King's Highways...

Lord Carslake of Northumberland and Enclosed Scenic Areas of Scotland: On a Point of Order, Prime Minister. Will my hon. Friend explain what in the name of galloping palsy 'macadamising' means?

Lord Cornwall of Cornwall: Aye, sir. It is the wilful ensmoothening of highways through the use of small stones laid within a binder of cement or asphalt, that carriages may pass more reliably, and at speed. Yet in whose interest is it that carriages may travel faster? Aye, in the interest of the Devil himself! All macadamised roads lead to Hell – to HELL I say, and they shall lead us there FASTER!

[Lord Cornwall raising his tankard aloft, losing his balance and falling. Hon. Members and Bailiffs attending, then raising him back to his seat and pressing upon him ardent spirits.]

The Prime Minister: My hon. Friend makes a strong and melancholy point. Alas, we cannot slow progress. Macadamisation is here to stay, for all we know with faster carriages upon them in the future. I recognise the hon. Member for Most of Cheshire.

Sir Wellington Flute (most of Cheshire): Sir, I wish to bring to the attention of the House the great increase of habitual drunkenness among the labouring classes of this kingdom, these deadly potions of ardent spirits in which the lower classes seem more than ever to indulge on their intoxicating march to DEATH. This may, in some measure, be attributed to the young not being taught to consider the practice disgraceful, and to their being tempted by the gorgeous splendour of the present gin-mansions.

Lord Peaty of Singlemalt: My hon. Friend is correct. If the labouring classes are able to access the world of ardent spirits and macadamised highways, what next, eh? Are they to share in our land, our meadows and ridings? Our WEALTH?

[Sharp intakes of breath, hon. Members steadying their nerves with ardent spirits, some accidental discharge of weapons, alarums & the Bailiffs summoning the Physician.]

FROM THE ARCHIVES: 1964

By the twentieth century society had moved on. Britain had become a more egalitarian, laid-back sort of place. Harold Wilson's government ushered in an exciting modern era. While there were those who embraced this new cultural landscape, full of technological advances, cultural upheaval and decriminalised sex, others deplored what they saw as a debasement of conservative values with certain brash new voices from the world of showbusiness. As we can see in this extract, some traditions remained, while others yielded to a novel and mischievous spirit.

The Chamber being assembled, the Great Door locked by the Bailiff of the House, a brief and reverent Silence for the Passing of Pre-Modern Britain. Then, three loud Knocks upon the Door.

The Great Door being opened, the prime minister (Mr Harold Wilson) entered in the company of the Beatles, all dressed in Parliamentary livery and cavorting in mockery of Pageantry and Procedure.

Mr George Harrison (A Beatle): It smells like me Nan's.

Mr John Lennon (A Beatle): Bring out your dead!

Mr Paul McCartney (A Beatle): Where's Ringo?

Hon. Members: Outrageous! Hear hear! It's them, it's the Swinging Blue Jeans! That's fab, that is! Gear! Get your bloody hair cut, you look like girls! Bailiffs, arrest them!

The Prime Minister: Mr Speaker, I wonder if I might prevail upon you to give way for a few minutes. It's just a bit of fun, that's all, to show that now the Labour party is in government we are in the cultural ascent once again.

The Leader of the Opposition (Sir Alec Douglas-Home): Philistine! Back to the North with you, you tiresome, squeaky-voiced little bugger.

The Prime Minister: Mr Speaker, I shall take no cheek from the Member opposite. He looks like one of those evil skeletons from that *Jason and the Argonauts* film.

Hon. Beatles: Yeah yeah yeah! He does though, yeah. Yeah.

Hon. Members: *tumult, tantrum, the offering of cigarettes, hon. Beatles signing Order Papers. Mr McCartney producing a guitar, indicating a sense of the situation being doubly swinging, his two thumbs erect.*

Mr McCartney *(singing, experimentally)*: Scrambled eggs... all my troubles seemed like scrambled eggs, now it looks as though they're scrambled eggs... oh I don't like these scrambled eggs...

The Speaker (Mr Richard Starkey): Order, order now! That scrambled eggs song is a drag, man. Tough crowd, and all. Let's move on. You, yeah. Feller with the pocket-watch and the cane and the top hat and the two dogs.

Mr Ezeriel Nowhere-Mann (Eastbourne Gallowsway): Hounds, dammit! These are hounds. Why, I've a good mind to give you and your fellow nancy-boys a sound thrashing. Mr Speaker – I want the real one for God's sake, not that blasted garden gnome – is this the shape of things to come? What next? Shall we lose our beloved capital punishment?

Hon. Members: Yes! No! Not sure!

Hon. Beatles: Off with his head! Hey, Bungalow Bill, what did you kill? Scrambled eggs!

Mr Ezeriel Nowhere-Mann: Are we to cast a compassionate eye upon beastly, depraved homo-sexualism?

Mr John Lennon: *(inaudible)* ... up them dogs of his.

Mr Ezeriel Nowhere-Mann: Should we desert our friends in the Commonwealth, struggling with the white man's burden, trying to keep a lid on savagery in far-away lands? Perhaps we should have more foreigners of all sorts, crowding into our cities, turning our civilisation into some damned carnival of bloody TOLERANCE!

Mr Enoch Powell (Wolverhampton Bloodfoam): Point of Order, Mr Speaker! My hon. Friend is wading into dangerous waters here. He knows full well that the content of his speech strays deeply into my private mind-world, where Trespassers Will Be Prosecuted. He must give way.

Hon. Members: *roaring, jeering, counter-jeering, growling, parping.*

Mr Ezeriel Nowhere-Mann: I will not, sir. I have not finished. Perhaps the Prime Minister intends to allow 'the ladies' more say!

Hon. Members: *(laughing)*

The Speaker: Orders, orders! Last orders, yeah?

Hon. Beatles: Four of fish and finger pie! Make mine a marshmallow one, dig it! Scrambled eggs!

Mrs. Barbara Castle (Addenough) then did seize the Ceremonial Mace and wielding it high brought it down upon the head of the hon. Member for Eastbourne Gallowsway, twice. Mrs. Castle then being restrained by the Bailiffs & medical aid summoned.

Mr McCartney: Hmm. Bang bang, something silver hammer, came down like I don't know, scrambled eggs...

FROM THE ARCHIVES: 2024

We move now into the twenty-first century, where proceedings in the Commons appear to be less unruly and yet more disrespectful. Here, a temporary prime minister knows he doesn't command the loyalty or indeed attention of much of the House. Once again, tradition endures, but subtle degradations in the ancient protocols are evident.

HOUSE OF COMMONS

Upon Wednesday 15th May 2024, Irritable Bowel Syndrome Awareness Day

PRAYERS, DRINKS AND NIBBLES

Mr Speaker in the Chair

Prime Minister's Googled Answer Time

The Chamber being assembled, the Great Door locked by the Bailiff of the House, a brief and reverent Silence for Privatised Utilities. Then, three loud Knocks upon the Door.

The Great Door being opened, the theme music to Succession *being broadcast upon an hi-fi. The Prime Minister then hurrying to the Opposition benches, consulting documents and in conversation upon his Blue-Tooth Apparatus.*

The Prime Minister (Mr Rishi Sunak): ... they're ceilinging it at two bil ... yes, ceilinging is a word, seriously, you think I'm some kind of idiaaaat, no YOU'RE the idiaaaat! Ha ha gotta go, Club Penguin EXACTLY yeah, yeah...

Hon Members: *Approbation, whistling, obscene heckling. The Prime Minister apprehending his mistake and taking his seat upon the Government front bench, for now.*

Mr Speaker: Order! Eh, eh, eh, order now, ye dafty barmcakes.

The Prime Minister (Mr Rishi Sunak): Yeah, check in later, gotta go, showtime, yeah I WILL fuck 'em up, ha ha yeah, hasta la vista baby!

Mr Noah Chancemate (Redwall Hairsbreadth): Would the Prime Minister list his engagements? And would he join me in [consulted prepared notes] 'saying something about Starmer. Like how the only engagement HE ever achieves is in a train toilet. Not that, but something like that. Then just shut the FUCK up and sit down again.' Oh, perhaps ignore the last bit...

Hon. Members: *cacophony, tumult, calls upon mobile telephones, the taking of cocaine, antics.*

Mr Speaker: Eh, eh, eh, eh, eh, order! Order. Pray silence for the Prime Minister.

The Prime Minister: Mr Speaker, this morning I met with Cabinet colleagues and – well, I say met, it was mostly WhatsApp, I was working on this start-up, oh by start-up I mean Start-Up For Britain, thoughtcloud, just spitballing. Treadmill, lunch was just a bit of lettuce and an iron tablet. Looked over some papers. Imports? Outports? Freeports? I won't be distracted, I have been clear about this.

[The prime minister then sitting down, checking his emails. Hon. Members half-heartedly muttering, sighing.]

Sir Keir Starmer (Leader of His Majesty's Opposition): *inaudible.*

Ms Angela Rayner (Ashton Undermine): Point of Order Mr Speaker, the Prime Minister's thick as Wythenshawe Tripe and spouting pure bollocks. Also, as a whatever, Emergency Motion, can we talk about DOGS, Mr Speaker. As I said on Instagram, our last-but-one prime minister looked like a fat gormless Dulux dog shagging the furniture didn't he, then his successor looked like one of them tiny yappy dogs posh bastards keep in their handbags. This one looks like a dopey dachshund who's just had his balls off. Are Staffy's got more brains, and SHE nearly had Kieran's step-mam's fucking HAND OFF!

Mr Speaker: Eh, eh, eh, eh! The hon. Lady will withdraw her vile and hateful remarks right now, or she can sling her blooming hook, I can tell her THAT for nowt!

Hon. Members: Yeah, outrageous! Woof woof! He DOES look like a neutered dachshund! You can talk, Rayner, you fucking panto horse!

Ms Angela Rayner: I heard that Kevin, you dickhead. Watch your back next time you're round ARE WAY.

Hon. Members: *contumely, sexual mimes.*

Ms Nadine Dorries (Air Bedfordshire): *[being restrained by Cudgellers]* He's not fat you cheap trollop, he's just

CONTOURED! If we were working class characters in a novel set in the nineteenth century, why lady I would fetch thee such a clout as thou—

Mr Speaker: Have we got blooming ORDER? HAVE we? Have we 'eck as like! Shut your pie-holes! I ask the hon. Lady again. Will she withdraw her remarks?

Ms Angela Rayner: Yeah yeah withdrawn, keep your girdle on Mr Speaker.

The Prime Minister: Apols, guys, gotta boost.

[The prime minister held his phone aloft by way of explanation.]

Sir Keir Starmer: *inaudible.*

Mr Speaker: Order, that's it! Drink up! Time, ladies and gentlemen please, you all have second homes to go to, I imagine.

The Prime Minister: *(outgoing, into mobile phone)* Yeah, July the Fourth, Independence Day. No YOU'RE a Wanky Doodle Dandy. Yes, I'm sure. No, it WON'T make me look 'wet', whatever that means.

In 1938, he returned from Munich with a piece of paper signed by Hitler, which massively helped to prevent World War II. Enemies with Lloyd George and, as it turned out, Hitler.

Neville CHAMBERLAIN

CONSERVATIVE
In office: 1937-1939

Months as PM	35
Largest Commons majority	242
Bullshit rating	8
Chaos factor	3
Legacy impact	3

Oversaw the Factories Act, which limited working hours, and the Holidays With Pay Act, which led to the advent of holiday camps. So made enemies of snobs too. Vibe: talking waxwork.

FROM THE IMAGINARY ARCHIVES: 2038

A sorry spectacle, we can all agree. But how would YOU handle the pressure of PMQs? Let's find out. We're moving forward to the near future. The Houses of Parliament were too costly to repair. They're now an interactive tourist destination, and the business of the House is conducted online, allowing MPs the freedom to make meaningful contributions in their pyjamas, without their wigs and make-up on. PMQs too is online, but it is still very much live, and many more people now monitor proceedings because they needn't put up with the ugly sound of raised voices. Over to you. Make sure to rope in a couple of your mates to be hon. Members, go off-script, get physically violent – you make the rules, you're the prime minister.

house of commons live feed

14 november, 2038

awareness days see full list...

moderator – bez khan

prime minister's AMA

virtual chamber assembled

access provided by INFOSYS

official silence sponsored by NHS PREMIUM

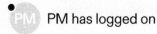 PM has logged on

---

MODERATOR: order, hi everyone. quick housekeeping note for democratic participants: be yourself, be kind to yourself and others, respectful engagement, have fun! hon mem 4 Islington Ocado...

HON MEM 34: hi PM, love you. what's been going on? Busy today?

PM (YOU):

MODERATOR: thx PM. hon mem 4 Preston OnlyFans...

HON MEM 185: yeah one of my lot paid >£4k for a knee fix, still waiting after 3 months. is this the new deal for NHS patients? Pay As You Wait? ha ha no joke

PM:

MODERATOR: yes, q here from hon mem 4 Exeter Apple Platinum...

HON MEM 244: the pm keeps telling us the economy's doing so *[deleted by mod]* well, why the *[deleted by mod]* are we selling norfolk to the *[deleted by mod]* chinese????

PM:

MODERATOR: pls keep comments in accordance with kindness and respect protocols. the hon mem 4 Sunderland Hitachi is suspended from session for INFRINGEMENT 3.05 FAECAL IMPROPRIETY. next q from hon mem 4 Basildon Safernet Solutions

HON MEM 601: with online fraud now the fourth largest economy in Britain, isn't it time we all made sure we have up-to-date protection? Safernet Solutions filters out the *[deleted by mod]*

HON MEM 529: point of order, will the PM tell this commons forum why we have not committed to UN emergency motion 38/04 on ecocide? we have to win the WAR ON CLIMATE TERROR we've already lost the Isle of Wight stop [deleted by mod] about and let's do somethinggggg

PM:

MODERATOR: last q from hon mem 4 Tamworth LG Airfilters

HON MEM 357: pm wat is yr fav inhalable alcoholic mist drink mine is atomised margarita

PM:

So how do you feel it went? You're not really a PM until you've weathered the shitstorm in the House of Commons. And the really great thing is that nobody ever remembers how well you did, so there's always next week to absolutely dazzle, you credulous political genius!

Took over from Chamberlain, headed National Government during World War II, during which he acquired mythical status. Famous for growling speeches, trademark cigar, V for Victory sign, boiler suit and being a much better painter than Hitler. Ousted by Labour in 1945, back as PM from in 1951.

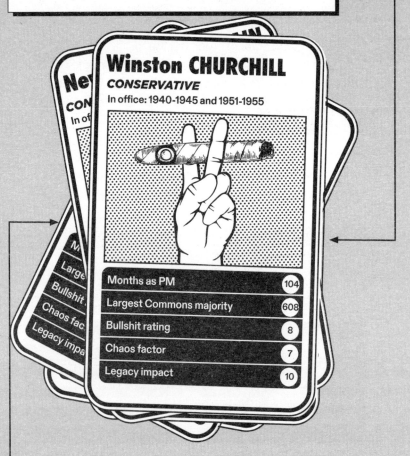

Winston CHURCHILL
CONSERVATIVE
In office: 1940-1945 and 1951-1955

Months as PM	104
Largest Commons majority	608
Bullshit rating	8
Chaos factor	7
Legacy impact	10

Second term conducted largely half-pissed in bed. Awarded Nobel Prize for Literature in 1953; voted Greatest-Briton of All Time in a 2002 BBC polls despite being half-American. Face like a bulldog; all bulldogs now look like Churchill. Vibe: irate allotment-holder.

It's time for...

FAMILY CHRISTMAS PMQS!

What you need:

A minimum of four players, two dice and this book. But it works better with as many people being rowdy backbenchers as possible.

What's it about?

Below are twelve entirely made-up and ridiculous proposed laws which the government is presenting for draft approval by the House of Commons. The prime minister is keen to rush these through with as little opposition as possible.

The prime minister's role in the game is to defend the policies. The leader of the opposition's role is to attack the policies. Both players should be as clever and funny as possible, deriding the other's position, criticising their attitude, their dress sense, their sexual attractiveness, their financial standing, their general demeanour, and so on. In many ways the exchange should be regarded as a sort of rap battle, but without the finesse or rhyming, unless everyone's feeling a little drunk and saucy and they reckon they can pull it off. If so, it is absolutely worth filming and putting online. The publisher of this book has promised a bottle of champagne for the best one. Good luck!

How to play

To allocate roles for the game, a die is cast in turn by each player until a 4, 5 and 6 have been thrown. The player who throws the 6 is the prime minister, 5 is the leader of the opposition and 4 is the Speaker. All other players will be hon. Members and should sort themselves into two teams of backbenchers. If there are only four players in total, the solitary hon. Member is free to keep changing their mind, or to be in charge of drinks.

To play the game, the opposition leader must throw two dice. If they throw a double 1, the number of the proposed law is one; if a double 3, the third proposed law is selected. If not a double, the face value of both dice determine the number of the law.

The Speaker then acknowledges the opposition leader and calls upon them to speak. They stand and address the House/ living room, for instance: 'Mr Speaker, does the prime minister realise that the proposed law to [...] is unthinkable and an affront to the people of Britain?' The leader of the opposition then goes on to argue the ways in which the law is unfair and cannot work, then sits down. The Speaker calls the prime minister to answer, and here everyone expects an escalation: not only does the PM defend the law, but they also criticise the opposition leader, tauntingly. The Speaker referees, calling each in turn to make their point, until it's time for a vote, or more drinks.

The Speaker must intervene if either the prime minister or the opposition leader has used unparliamentary language. The following words have been deemed unparliamentary over time: bastard, blackguard, coward, deceptive, dodgy, drunk, falsehoods, git, guttersnipe, hooligan, hypocrite, idiot, ignoramus, liar, misled, pipsqueak, rat, slimy, sod, squirt, stool pigeon, swine, tart, traitor, and wart. Yes, it's an eclectic list, and no, just because it's not on the list doesn't mean you're allowed to call your opponent a fucking prick.

Any suggestion that someone is lying to the House or on the take should prompt a warning from the Speaker, followed by expulsion from the game. There's an apocryphal story about Dennis Skinner, the former MP for Bolsover who – in legend, anyway – pointed to the Conservative benches and said half of them were crooks. He was immediately called upon by the Speaker to withdraw and said 'Okay, half the Members opposite are NOT crooks.'

The Speaker must show authority – in this game, at least – and the players could agree on the level of brutality allowed before the game starts. Perhaps one infringement incurs a smack with a rolled-up magazine; the second a kick in the leg and expulsion from the game, with a new dice-throw to determine a replacement.

THE PROPOSED LAWS TO BE DEBATED

His Majesty's Government proposes the following law, to:

 Redefine NHS waiting lists as 'initial procedure schedules' so that anyone waiting for a procedure is deemed to have begun their treatment by being theoretically ready for it well in advance, thus reducing waiting lists to zero.

 Ban the use of mobile phones – except for emergency calls – by anyone over the age of seventy, in order to reduce public nuisance and general irritation.

 Require all runners on paths, walkways, towpaths, pavements and other public pedestrian routes to carry a bell, to be sounded as a warning to pedestrians being approached from behind, in order to alert them to the runner's approach and avert their face from the inevitable guffed cloud of phlegmy microdroplets containing fuck knows what.

 Establish a Pet Shit Database. All cats and dogs to be registered at birth and DNA samples taken. A free app to be available to allow users to scan and geolocate offending pet shit, identify the pet and its registered owner, with courts empowered to impose a fine and/or require the owner to eat the pet shit.

 Solve the 'North–South divide' by reversing the polarity on all maps, thus levelling up Scotland and the North with a congenial 'southern location' and elevating the northernised South with more much-needed compensatory cash incentives.

 Equalise the age of eligibility for a state pension so that men and women both start receiving it at 92.

7 Make it illegal for any car hi-fi system to be audible outside the vehicle, and to make compulsory a requirement for all new cars to be fitted with a decibel-activated immobiliser and automatic ejector seat to expel the gratifyingly startled arsehole with his sleeve tattoo and footballer's haircut into oncoming traffic.

8 Criminalise homework from January next year, to make it illegal for children to be given extra work to do at home, to require schools to teach what they can during the day and leave students to find out anything else they want to know on the fucking internet, like everybody else.

9 Introduce as soon as possible a three-day working week for all occupations, from Tuesday to Thursday, and to formalise a four-day weekend, with all current wages and salaries unaffected and any losses to be absorbed by employers.

10 Legalise all drugs, impose VAT on retail sales subject to rigorous quality testing, and make everything available at pharmacies and off-licences.

11 Bring back the rationing of meat, with strict allowances imposed per person, to be reduced gradually year on year towards a Meat-Free Britain by 2050. #MeatZero50

12 Abolish parliamentary recognition of the Leader of the Opposition, in order to hasten business in the House, and to have Prime Minister's Questions emanate solely from government backbenchers, thus removing rancour from proceedings and allowing the prime minister to get on with actually governing the country rather than chat shit with the hon. Member opposite.

The most boring man in political history somehow wrangled a bunch of rowdy maniacs into the most transformative government of the century. It's as if a traffic warden got the Beatles together. Between 1945 and 1951, the Attlee crew created a post-war settlement that was to last three decades.

Clement ATTLEE

LABOUR

In office: 1945-1951

Months as PM	75
Largest Commons majority	146
Bullshit rating	2
Chaos factor	1
Legacy impact	10

They set up the NHS, nationalised major industries and public utilities, expanded social services, created the welfare state, secondary education for all, university scholarships, school meals, free school milk, set up the Arts Council, oversaw the decolonisation of India, Pakistan, Burma, Ceylon and Jordan. They were fully behind the creation of Israel. The *Windrush* arrived in 1948 and Attlee had to swat away opposition to immigration from his own Labour MPs. Margaret Thatcher, who was to dismantle much of Attlee's work, said of him: 'He was all substance and no show.' Vibe: suburban Lenin-alike.

PMQs WORD SEARCH

P	O	I	N	T	O	F	O	R	D	E	R	E
I	A	S	G	P	I	P	S	Q	U	E	E	E
P	O	R	D	E	R	X	R	E	D	O	B	E
S	E	A	R	B	C	U	S	H	L	R	M	A
Q	Q	F	U	A	I	M	B	E	V	G	E	Y
U	A	E	W	K	N	H	X	H	K	R	M	U
E	P	A	I	L	I	N	G	E	N	E	N	H
A	Z	I	U	I	E	X	A	H	O	A	O	A
K	N	X	Q	G	W	S	P	E	D	T	H	A
G	W	P	C	F	L	T	I	H	K	D	E	A
H	E	I	B	A	I	L	I	F	F	O	N	E
E	F	H	E	A	R	H	E	A	R	O	F	G
B	A	C	K	B	E	N	C	H	O	R	P	X

ORDER	☐	EEEAYUHAA ☐
PIPSQUEAK	☐	HONMEMBER ☐
BAILIFF	☐	GREATDOOR ☐
BACKBENCH	☐	POINTOFORDER ☐
HEARHEAR	☐	EHEHEHEH ☐

PART TWO

So, now you've seen how everything works in theory, it's time to put that hard-earned knowledge into practice. Time to make a plan, begin your journey to the top job, lose your way a bit, retrace your steps, throw the original plan away, start again and so on until you make it, even if you end up worn out, really bad-tempered and arsey.

CHAPTER 4:
IT'S PARTY TIME!

Political profiling, like charity, begins at home. Think about your extended family: all those poorly composed, unfocused photographs in the Quality Street tin. Which family member do you admire most, and from which era? If it's your gran in the 1980s, you might, for example, like the current Labour party. If you like the look of your grandad in the 1960s, maybe the Conservative party's right for you. That blurry little black-and-white Kodak of your unsmiling great-grandfather on Southend beach c.1956: check out Reform, that's very much their vibe. Admiring the mature fashion choices of Auntie Mavis in the 1990s? The Lib Dems might welcome your interest.

There are tough choices to make, voting in a liberal democracy that's already a quarter of the way through the twenty-first century. Should you perhaps choose a party that aligns with your principles? Obviously you need a political party to be PM, so if you don't belong to one, you should join one now. Is there a party you feel drawn to ideologically? In that case, you need to forget all about that ideological alignment as soon as possible. It's much more important to find a party that's drawn to YOU.

Politics Is Serious – So Shop Around

First things first, do you have scruples? YES: oh dear. Google all the political parties, see whose policies are a good fit, maybe? NO: great, let's find the fastest route.

Assuming you're interested primarily in becoming prime minister, and only marginally in how you get there, you need to think about a political party not as a potential spiritual home, but as one of several political bidders. They're all after the special value you might add to their organisation.

In the last century, people gravitated to one party or another because they represented their very clear class interest. They rose through the party, from member to activist, from representative to leader. Weird now to think of a House of Commons packed – as it was generations ago – on one side by shop stewards and socialists of humble origins, on the other by officers and landowners. These days it's all lawyers and journalists and business owners or increasingly people who've been in political roles (special advisers, local or regional councillors) since university and have only really known that world. There are those who would argue that this weakens the link between politicians and ordinary people, and that this is a bad thing. But is it? Not if you're in a hurry to become prime minister.

A culture that reveres instant celebrity and favours distracted scrolling over focused understanding is ideal for the politician who's not that into actual politics. Gone are the days of true-blue Tories or Labour-for-lifers. At the time of writing, a sitting MP has gone from Labour to Tory to Reform in the space of six years. He hasn't changed his views, he's just found a pathway across parties that emboldens him to express them in ever more colourful and explicit terms. And let's not forget that a youthful Lib Dem activist became, fleetingly, a Conservative prime minister. You are entirely at liberty to make your mark, use the most convenient party as a ladder, then hop to a better one when you need to. You're political capital, in a seller's market.

Why Would a Party Want You?

That depends. What have you got to offer? Maybe you have money, in which case a) brilliant but b) why in the name of corrugated fuck would you go into politics? Are you driven by the thought that you might change things for the better? Fair enough, it's your life. And if you're rich and political, you're halfway there. Just as parties are always on the lookout for donors, candidates who can bankroll their own brand recognition are regarded as quite the attractive article.

Even better, if you're rich and idealistic and politics is calling you, whoa Nelly: you've just cleared a pathway to political fame. To be idealistic, of course, you needn't be a 'let's scrap Trident, abolish the home office, free 80 per cent of prisoners and nationalise fresh air and rainbows' type, at all. You could be a 'let's start stockpiling nuclear weapons, fully militarise the police, aggressively hold on to and expand the Commonwealth, by force if necessary – we're British, we're ambitious and we want our Empire back!' type. Just probably don't expect to be welcomed with open arms by every party.

Perhaps you're... popular? You've built a reputation for yourself outside the world of politics, and a party could really use some of that reflected popularity. Actors, musicians, TV personalities – all can bring across with them a fandom that automatically makes any party look slightly younger, more attractive, sexier and more electable. The sort of party that draws admiring looks from the electorate, who may wonder aloud if the party in question has lost weight recently because they tell it what, it looks bloody tremendous.

Perhaps you have local clout, or you're a location-specific celebrity. You may have led a campaign to save a hospital from closure, or you prevented the felling of some ancient woodland. The advantage here is that your local reputational heft is of great interest to political parties, who may value your maverick can-do stubbornness, or your community conscience. Let's face it, depends who they are. The disadvantage is that you have to save a hospital or a forest, and honestly that stuff can be a real time-suck.

Here's a more radical approach: remain a wildcard, a free spirit, an independent. That might get you the MP's job, from where you can leap to an existing party happy to have you. Once in, you can go into full parasite-host mode. Attach yourself to the fringe of a party, become its figurehead, push it to extreme lunacy, take over and consume the host party, then crowdsurf your way to ultimate power: the Trump Model Strategy. Or maybe, if you're feeling super-confident, stay exactly where you are and wait for defectors from other parties to join yours.

In office he presided over the Swinging Sixties from 1964 to 1970, then back for the Static Seventies from 1974 to 1976. Abolished capital punishment and theatre censorship, relaxed laws on homosexuality, divorce, abortion. Increased top rate of tax to 83%, substantially improved conditions for low-paid. Set up the Open University.

Harold WILSON
LABOUR
In office: 1964-1970 and 1974-1976

Months as PM	93
Largest Commons majority	98
Bullshit rating	8
Chaos factor	3
Legacy impact	7

Expanded welfare state with increased spending on education, health and social housing. Carefully cultivated image as 'man of the people' with his Gannex raincoat and pipe (he preferred cigars, but that would have made him look like a capitalist). Bugged by MI5. In 1969 sent troops to Northern Ireland, with extremely mixed results. Ill health forced his retirement in 1976, with Alzheimer's already in the post. Vibe: encyclopaedia salesman.

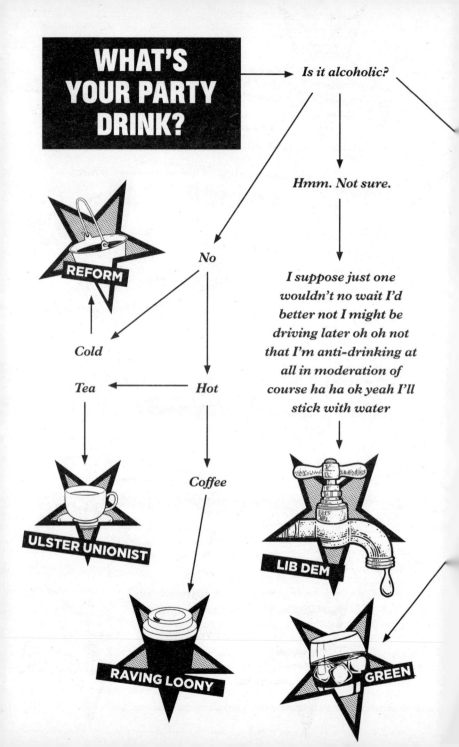

WHAT'S YOUR PARTY DRINK?

Is it alcoholic?

Hmm. Not sure.

No

REFORM

Cold

I suppose just one wouldn't no wait I'd better not I might be driving later oh oh not that I'm anti-drinking at all in moderation of course ha ha ok yeah I'll stick with water

Tea ← *Hot*

Coffee

ULSTER UNIONIST

LIB DEM

RAVING LOONY

GREEN

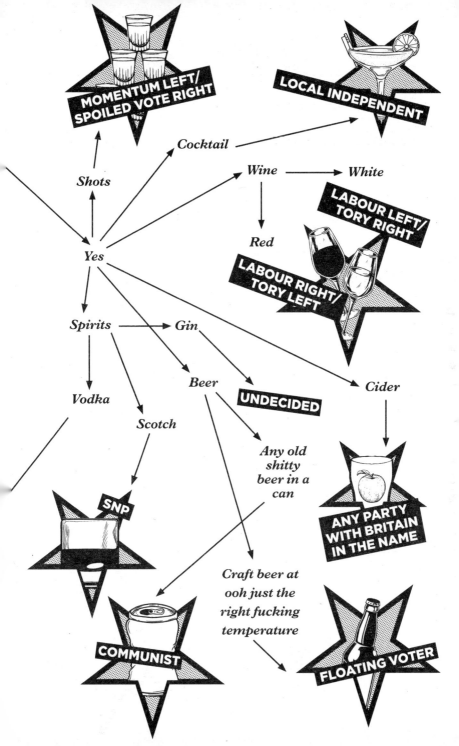

CRISIS AT QUIZMAS

Take this short multiple-choice Crisis Quiz to determine which party is right for you to join, infiltrate, dominate and lead to victory in a general election. Your choice of answer for each Crisis Solution will reveal your true political self. What are you: despot or doormat, or somewhere between? Team player or solo artist? Here we go...

The Climate Crisis

A | *So what do these Just Stop Oil wankers want to do with all that oil and coal that's left? 'Leave it in the ground.' Brilliant. I'll just leave my dinner in the shop, shall I? I'll just leave my trousers on the floor, shall I? GROW UP. I was brought up to believe Earth's Natural Resources are just that: resources. The bloody hot weather brigade would have us all living in mud huts doing the* Guardian *crossword. NOT IN MY NAME. Drill, frack, burn it up, let's all have a barbeque with our tops off.*

B | *We owe it to our children and to our children's children, and to all children ad infinitum, to save the world from certain destruction. The Arctic Circle is on fire. There are unprecedented storms and heatwaves. Wildlife is dying. Crops are dying. We're three catastrophes away from water wars. We need to insulate, invest heavily in sustainable energy, and go vegetarian. Vegan, ideally. Walk everywhere, or bicycle if we're feeling haughty. We must curb all emissions, whether they originate from a human chimney or a cow's arse. Save the Earth!*

C | *We need to balance Net Zero aspirations with more appropriate energy management. Let's get there, but not at a speed that hurts the economy. More trees, more heat pumps, more jumpers in the winter, sensible precautions, steady improvement is the way forward, gently does it.*

Artificial Intelligence generators will soon need as much water as South Korea. Cryptocurrency servers use as much power as South Korea again, probably. Two South Koreas' worth. And who's responsible for this arse ache? Slightly balding men in their thirties who all live in those see-through Modernist houses. Let's start by culling those fuckers and busk it from there.

The Cost of Living Crisis

A   *'Cost of Living'? We should rename this the PRICE of living. If you don't want to pay it, then fine – die. Everyone knows things have been getting steadily more expensive since the Norman Conquest, when a three-bedroom house cost a farthing or whatever. People call it a 'crisis' because they simply don't want to work hard. My advice is stop buying fancy food and make your own coffee or even better, good old-fashioned cocoa. The 'Sound of Whingeing' Crisis, more like.*

B   *Hard-working families are at the mercy of price-fixing by commercial cartels and cheated by shrinkflation: they're paying more and getting less. This will not do, which is why I believe we should nationalise capitalism itself. Food banks do sterling work, but the very concept is a stain on the character of our nation. Food banks should be nationalised too, along with money itself and families, probably – let's have a clean sweep.*

C   *This country, once famed for its farming, needs food security. It feels wrong to be eating veg flown in from African countries. We need an urgent inquiry into food, fuel and energy policies. The customer has to come first. Rising prices disproportionately affect the poorest, and that must change as a matter of urgency.*

D   *Just move the decimal point one place to the left, so a litre of milk costs 10p and a decent used car costs a grand. Also, 'pay what you can afford' for gas and electricity.*

The National Health Service Crisis

A | *Too much waste, too many strikes, too much corporate laziness. Our health delivery system was designed for a smaller population who died younger in those days, in an entirely different world. I'm not saying the NHS is full of freeloaders and incompetents and that it should be floated on the stock market without delay. I mean, other people are though, and we should listen to them.*

B | *The NHS is the jewel in Britain's crown. Remember the dancing nurses in the 2012 London Olympics opening ceremony? Nurses should be dancing all the time. Reform? Yes, of course, things could be more efficient. But no privatisation, not even to clear waiting lists. That would be a betrayal of our great-grandparents who, okay, are dead, but still. Protect our NHS at all costs! Let our nurses dance!*

C | *It is time to take a hard and pragmatic look at how the NHS functions, how it is funded, how it may be improved. The fundamental principle of a service free at the point of delivery must be preserved. But let's at least investigate the possibility of private-sector backlog clearance. Also, if commercial companies get to have a go at simple and very lucrative cataract operations, let's see if we can't persuade them — legally with full force — to take on some A&E backlog operations, for instance. That seems only fair.*

D | *End the NHS postcode lottery by making treatment available via an actual lottery. A £2 ticket gives you a one-in-a-hundred chance to win anything from a doctor's appointment to a chest X-ray or, if you're really lucky, palliative care. Unwanted procedures can be sold on eBay, lottery proceeds will fund the NHS: simple.*

The Immigration Crisis

A | *Zero tolerance. Migrants arriving on small boats should be sent back immediately on even smaller boats. Anyone on the olive—treacle tone spectrum should be refused entry to this country unless they're here for a family holiday or a paid-for term at a university. Also, anyone caught talking on a mobile phone in a foreign language should face jail time. Also, no funny hats, etc.*

B | *Humane management. There's no such thing as an illegal migrant, and refugees should in any case be treated with compassion. Resources should be poured into immigration processing and management. Every 'crisis' is an opportunity. Let's get the adults to work as quickly as possible: this is exactly the productivity boost the economy needs. Welcome the boats! Let Britain be a beacon for the future!*

C | *This whole issue is incredibly complex and emotionally loaded. The British People deserve a serious examination of the pros and cons, including a dispassionate impact assessment and a realistic forecast of numbers. I shall push for an urgent debate, free from the self-serving rhetoric and hatred that so often obscures this important matter.*

D | *Make all migration traffic one-way, the way they do on narrow roads. So all migrants may travel in one direction only through designated countries (such as France–England–Scotland–Wales–Ireland–Iceland), picking up valuable 'migrant tokens' as they go, then when they've got, say, a thousand they can stay where they are. Just a thought.*

The Housing Crisis

A | *Do you know how many spare rooms this country has, in houses up and down the land, above shops, in woefully underused sheds? A lot. Where's the bulldog spirit of yesteryear, when everybody had a lodger and we all made do with fishpaste sandwiches and loose-leaf tea? Everyone needs to budge up a bit. Not On My Nearest Area Of Green Belt Or Golf Course should be our, admittedly quite convoluted, watchword.*

B | *The scandalously low level of housebuilding in recent years has a direct knock-on effect on rents (exorbitant) and homelessness (unacceptable). The whole economy should be geared to producing more dwellings than we actually need, just in case people drop in unannounced. Houses and flats should be sustainable, carbon-neutral, energy-efficient and ridiculously cheap. Everyone needs to spread out a bit. It's a simple choice: hooray Henrys guffawing at the eighteenth hole and living in mansions in the countryside that lie empty for tax purposes most of the time, or a decent kitchen for your nan. Or toilet, if that's more urgent.*

C | *We need to produce more good-quality social housing, look carefully at a fair land tax system, examine the case for rent caps and try to ease the burden on young people especially, who have none of the advantages their boomer grandparents enjoyed. We owe our children decent homes, and maybe a bit of lawn or a vegetable patch. Window boxes at the very least.*

D | *Ideas: horizontal skyscrapers (easier to build). Squatting decriminalised if they went to university. Encourage innovative residential development, e.g. inflatable social housing around the Isle of Man, tent cities in disused Wilko supermarkets, converted shipping containers along hard shoulder of the M6.*

The Shit Crisis

A | *Within living memory, certainly if you're very old and can still remember, the River Thames was a poisonous, filthy deathtrap. Nobody minded then — some perspective please. Shit is about the most 'natural' thing there is; nature will sort it out. I say give the shareholders a break.*

B | *Nationalisation of our public utilities has been a disaster. Money has been steadily gushing out for years, from taxpayers and consumers to fat cats and shareholders. Bonuses for failing CEOs is a disgrace. Shit is in the sea around our beautiful British coastline and in our rivers and streams. Swimming and surfing — even the Boat Race — is hazardous. Stop all dividends and bonuses, give us our clean water back. Now. Thanks.*

C *Renationalisation would be hugely expensive and would not guarantee a speedy return to the clean seas and rivers we all want to see. We need to set targets and deadlines, hold the water companies to their promises to improve. And obviously to take all sensible precautions near water, including not going in it.*

D *Enough. Renationalise. Claw back all dividends and bonuses paid in the last ten years. Impose a lifetime hosepipe ban on shareholders and hook up raw sewage to the jacuzzis and swimming pools of executives.*

Answers on page 239

CHAPTER 5:
NO CAMPAIGN, NO GAIN

Dance for your country

Having the public on your side is always helpful when you have a political career to build. But let's be honest, most of the time they're a bit of a pain, aren't they? The endless demands, the tedious petitions and campaigns, the constant moaning about their horrible landlord and the price of rail fares and how they can never get a GP appointment. As if any of that is your fault. You're just a politician, for God's sake!

The public are only really useful at election time, when they can demonstrate their usefulness by voting for you and your party. Even then it's not like the old days, when everybody smoked and everybody voted. Nowadays turnout at general elections is around two-thirds of the electorate, and local elections are an altogether bleaker affair. Several county councillors in East Anglia are only there because they remembered at the last moment to vote for themselves.

Voting's just not very congenial, is it? Now people have to take photo ID with them, as if they're applying for a visa just to remain part of a democracy. Even worse, the whole pantomime takes place in some genuinely dreadful polling stations. These are terminally melancholic spaces: a 'safe enough' section of a crumbling school, a local church haunted by the afterlife of faith, a parish hall smelling vaguely of over-60s aerobics and Cub Scouts.

Although it has to be said that these places are often enlivened by the presence of dogs outside. In recent years it has become fashionable for people to share pictures of Dogs At Polling Stations on social media. In many ways the democratic process is more vividly illustrated by dogs than it is by voters, who are much less friendly and have a uniformly defeated look about them.

There are two key election campaigns that stand between You The Vaguely Motivated Citizen and You The Ass-Kicking Boss of Westminster: local and national. First, you need to be an MP, which means getting selected by your party of choice, finding a good seat to contest, or a constituency you feel an emotional attachment to, running a good local campaign, winning the seat, ascending through the party like an upwardly mobile parasite, becoming leader, heading a brilliant national campaign, becoming PM.

First PM to be appointed by Queen Elizabeth, although he was sceptical of monarchy and wanted to keep Lilibet Windsor out of politics. He took over in 1955 when Churchill retired and stayed long enough to be the face of national humiliation over the Suez crisis.

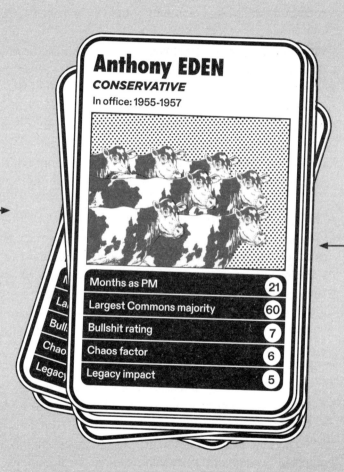

Anthony EDEN
CONSERVATIVE
In office: 1955-1957

Months as PM	21
Largest Commons majority	60
Bullshit rating	7
Chaos factor	6
Legacy impact	5

Egypt's nationalisation of the canal exposed Britain's loss of imperial power, his health crumbled, he resigned. In retirement he tended a herd of 60 Herefordshire cattle, the same number as his majority. Vibe: baffled vicar.

Location, Location, Et Cetera

Assuming you've settled on a party (see Chapter 4 if you still want to faff about a bit longer like a dithering chimp), you can now start to shop around to find a good fit geographically. Constituency parties like to feel they've selected someone with a strong connection to the area, perhaps someone who grew up there. If you're a perfect prospective candidate otherwise, though, accommodations can always be made.

What, after all, is a local connection anyway? It's a sliding scale from 'lived here all my life' to 'popped into T K Maxx on the way'. You may have decided on a political party to represent, which means finding a constituency you fancy. Maybe it IS where you live, which would certainly simplify the backstory.

Of course, if party allegiance isn't important, you can simply zero in on a constituency you like and join the party that gives you the best shot at becoming MP. People might accuse you of taking an overly cynical view of politics, but that's just because they haven't spent much time actually in politics.

First among losers

You need to be selected to get elected, as nobody says, ever. As long as you've been a member of the party for a while (usually between three months and a year) you're good to go. Once you've persuaded the party to put you on the shortlist – you're keen, you're loyal, your beliefs accord resoundingly with theirs, whatever they may be at election time – it's up to you how you convince the constituency party to choose you over the pathetic shower of losers you're up against. Your potential rivals may include the following:

★ Son/daughter of outgoing MP retiring due to age/ burgeoning scandal

★ Intense librarian who can recite the names of every local council member since 1794

★ Middle-class early retiree in a pastel jumper whose 'passion is politics'

★ Local housebuilder and developer interested in simplifying the planning system

★ Student with elaborate neck tattoo who can't face a second term at university

★ Constituency party stalwart who has persuaded colleagues to 'persuade them to stand'

Of all these, the last one is clearly your biggest threat, as they will have the overwhelming support of the very people choosing the candidate. You must undermine them not with crude smear tactics, but with slightly more sophisticated ones. Some ideas:

★ Have stationery confidently printed up with their name followed by 'MP' delivered to the constituency office

★ Leave a breathless, detailed review for a sex harness in their name at swingfuck.com

★ Reveal a series of anonymous threats addressed to you, which sound an awful lot like them

★ Secure an endorsement for them from a convicted fraudster

★ Arrange to have partially pixellated dick pics delivered to target addresses. On the back: 'Nobody needs to see this. Vote [your rival prospective candidate's name] to stop unacceptable porn spam!'

Candidate night

Now you've been selected as the party candidate, your next goal is to stand with a group of strangers on a makeshift stage in a leisure centre, waiting for the result confirming that you're an MP. Some of these people – your rival candidates – will be serious people wearing normal clothes. Others will be chancers and piss-takers wearing Druid costumes or a bin on their head or entirely enclosed within a giant egg.

You're about to win. You'll be duly elected MP, either because your party has for years enjoyed an obliterating majority, or because you and your election agent have run a barnstorming campaign, compelling in its argument that you are the representative this constituency needs and deserves.

The lessons you have learned in becoming an MP will be invaluable when the time comes for the general election, when you and the party you lead will stand on a much bigger makeshift stage, celebrating victory over a political enemy out of ideas and time. There they go, the sniffling losers, shuffling towards the exit, petulantly tearing off their rosettes. By the time you lead your party to a general election win you will be building on your campaign strength locally and adding some national campaign strategies. Let's start with some basics.

Call your agent

Your election agent is the person legally responsible for the conduct of your political campaign, and who makes sure your campaign spending is above board. You can be your own election agent if you want to spend weeks filling in forms and making sure your own behaviour is impeccable. But it's often better to let other, sympathetic, supportive people be the judge of whether your conduct is within the law and act as your agent instead.

When you and your agent are planning your campaign you'll be tested with the following dilemma. Is the forthcoming election about promoting your strengths as a candidate, or is it about smearing your opponents with the worst possible accusations in a brutal attempt to destroy their character as far as possible, pushing the concept of acceptable conduct to its very limits? Trick question, the answer is both of course.

Your campaign should be a bracing affair, rising above the tired and unimaginative traditional forms of communication. But it's often better to let other, sympathetic, supportive people be the judge of whether your conduct is within the law and act as your agent instead.

Your campaign should be a bracing affair, rising above the tired and unimaginative traditional forms of communication.

Weaponised leaflets

The traditional, and frankly very boring, way of telling your prospective constituents who you are and what you notionally stand for is through leafletting. Not for the first time, you will need a plucky little army of weirdos prepared to walk around your target constituency, pushing your propaganda through letterboxes with their trusty wooden spatulas so they don't lose a finger to an over-snappy return mechanism or a stir-crazy Alsatian.

A leaflet rarely has impact, as you have to get your message across in the ten seconds between someone picking it up and tossing it in the bin. A convention in recent years is to have the layout mimic a local newspaper. This has been hugely successful, as most papers, like most leaflets, are dull and poorly written. Most conventional leaflets include the following:

★ Several low-definition photos of the candidate in the same clothes, smiling in different locations with groups of volunteers who clearly think litter-picking is hilarious

★ Wads of generic fluff from central office about irrelevant national policies

★ At least one blurry photo of the candidate in ill-fitting hi-vis tabard and hard hat pointing at something

★ A five-point plan from central office headed 'PRIORITIES FOR [INSERT CONSTITUENCY]' because nobody's checked the headline

★ A web address for the local party office that starts 'http://www.' as nothing much has changed since 1996

You need to make your leaflets interesting enough for people to read more than three words before binning it. You could, for example, have them folded in such a way that the first thing the recipient sees is:

And then they open it up, and it goes on to say...

Yeah, you're right, it IS still very 'campaign leaflet'. You need to make your leaflets PROPERLY different, for example:

★ Have them scented. Suggestions: cut grass, kebab, pine car freshener, weed, strawberry vape
★ Candidate's name and party printed in edible ink on carrots, along with the slogan 'crunch time'
★ Name and party printed on a bin bag, with the slogan 'On Election Day, help me take out the trash'
★ On one side, a big question mark. On the other, a website address. There, the candidate (you, being brilliant) answers questions such as 'Why should the voting age be lowered to sixteen?' and 'Have you ever taken Class A drugs?' and 'Do we really need a royal family?' in a variety of stunning outfits

ON ELECTION DAY, HELP ME TAKE OUT THE TRASH!

VOTE
CANDIDATE NAME HERE

[GENERIC GUFF]

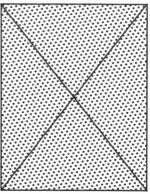

FIVE POINT PLAN:

1. --
2. --
3. --
4. --
5. --

Blank canvassing

As part of your successful campaign, teams of canvassers will be needed to face ordinary people and their blunt questions, and deliver vague generic-but-cheerful answers.

Why? Because contact with the right kind of canvasser can significantly increase voter turnout, sometimes by more than 10 per cent if you're unlucky and householders, enraged by your shiny-faced door-knockers, think 'fuck this, I'm voting against their guy just for the vengeance'.

Your canvassers should always be in pairs. It's easier this way to deal with a belligerent malcontent who blames politics for everything wrong in his life – his divorce, his unemployed status, his shitty house with the doorbell that doesn't work so people have to bang on the door, and now the canvassers who are being specifically blamed and threatened in detail. If canvassers are in twos, canvasser one can pull away canvasser two, who's actually totally up for a one-on-one with this angry arsehole who looks well out of shape. Also, two canvassers make it easier to keep a conversation going, especially if one of them is still muttering about how he'd totally win that fight.

The most useful canvassing does several things at once:

★ Gathers information on the disposition of an area and its inhabitants, including socio-economic profile, Pothole Index score, the prevalence of dangerous dogs, TV volumes, kempt-garden quotient, ambient smells

★ Offers help to potential voters, such as lifts to polling stations, advice on who might be a good person to vote for, giving on-the-spot 'reads' of a householder's outfit, demeanour or sass quotient, the way they do on *RuPaul's Drag Race*

★ Raises awareness about an issue. Do they know, for instance, that your candidate is promising more GPs for the area and free Wetherspoons breakfasts, and also that they're definitely the candidate to vote for?

Canvassers should ideally be young and very good-looking. They should observe basic dress rules: no visible piercings, no obscene T-shirts and strictly no smoking, not even spliffs. They should be open, and notice things on their approach that might break the ice before sliding into the political stuff. Things like 'Oh I love your hanging basket' or 'Ha! My uncle Paul has an old fridge in his front garden too! Snap! Have you done time as well?'

Canvassers try to find a human story they can connect to your canvassing message. They should find out what issues the householder feels are important, and then try to draw them in. So, for instance, if a canvassee mentions that they're worried about getting old and being alone and needing medical treatment that might not be available because of lengthening NHS waiting lists, your canvassers could respond with their own stories, and hint at how their candidate (you, let's not forget) will deal urgently with this. Perhaps something sympathetic like this: 'Oh, I don't blame you. My poor old mum was a martyr to her arthritis, on a two-year waiting list. Too late in the end, she died of a heart attack before an appointment could be arranged. But I know our candidate is very keen to smooth the way for assisted dying so perhaps you'll suffer less when the same thing happens to you... oh, and you know they want to build a motorway by-pass? Well we're fighting for that too!'

Canvassers should be made aware as a matter of urgency of the 'no tea' rule. If householders invite them in for a cup of tea THEY MUST NOT ENTER THE PROPERTY. This is a ruse. In extremely rare cases the householder is a serial killer, but it's much more likely they're Jehovah's Witnesses. During an election period, when door-knocking suddenly increases, Witnesses know that people's tolerance for answering the doorbell is at its lowest. So the more canny Jehovah's Witnesses, as well as the naturally lazier ones, will do what's known in evangelical circles as 'reverse-canvassing'. Once you're settled in with a much-needed cup of tea and a Hobnob, you'll obviously want to talk about the candidate. So will they. About theirs. 'Do you know who DID poll quite badly locally but who then DID come back from the dead and WAS elected to higher office?' they will ask you, and by now you'll realise you're there for at least the duration of a cup of tea and a Hobnob, with only your fellow canvasser for support. That's why Jehovah's Witnesses always knock in pairs too. Support.

The Great British Face-Off

All of the above will yield valuable lessons for the REAL vote of your life. Once you've elbowed your valued and supportive colleagues and competitors out of the way to become party leader, don't forget that you still have to win a general election.

Yes, you'll show your face in that constituency you won four years ago, but now the stakes are much, much higher. But don't get too full of yourself: remember the Dull Triumph of 1992...

Is your party expected to win a majority? If yes, don't get complacent. The Labour party is haunted by the memory of its legendary Sheffield Rally, held a week ahead of the 1992 general election. Strategists had been planning it for eighteen months, which was the first mistake. Or maybe the second. The first was probably having Neil Kinnock – a Welsh windbag with a combover and the demeanour of a petty tyrant – as party leader.

Despite polling that showed Labour would win but with a small majority, or perhaps deliver only a hung Parliament, a massive presidential-style rally went ahead at the Sheffield Arena, attended by the entire Shadow Cabinet and 10,000 party members. Kinnock was choppered in like some white, freckled version of Prince. He strode through the cheering hall to Queen's 'We Are the Champions', leapt onto the stage, roared 'Well, all RIGHT!' into the mic repeatedly, in the style of a rock and roll MC, and led a surge of exaltation celebrating Labour's election victory in advance. They lost.

Is your party expected to lose the election? Then it needs to lean hard on its secret weapon: you. Of course, you're charismatic, an exceptional person. But maybe your chief rival – the leader of the party that's expected to win – is too.

Here the 1992 general election also gives valuable pointers. Despite a recession, a rise in crime and an expected Tory defeat, the Conservatives played their trump card: John Major, the most boring person in the western hemisphere. He was so dull he was routinely portrayed in satirical greyscale. Yet despite the Tories' disastrous polling as a party, Major, the ordinary bloke who liked plain food and had the voice of a Muppet, consistently outpolled Kinnock. People preferred Major as prime minister. The Tories won.

Remember: sometimes it's not a question of outflanking your

opponent from the left or right, but from the boring side. Your media manager and comms team can show you how to be less interesting. They can also advise you on something that would have been utterly unimaginable in 1992...

A Robust Social Media Strategy

This would once have seemed a weird priority, especially in the time before the internet, when 'social media', if it meant anything at all, meant going to the cinema with your friends, rather than having high-energy arguments with total strangers.

A social media strategy needs to be really well thought out. But not by you. This sort of thing is best done in a way that offers you plausible deniability if it all goes tits up. Because a great deal of infantile mischief may be had, especially if your social media team are all under twenty-five and have no idea what politics is.

Yes, by 'really well thought out', your social media team actually means 'ill-conceived and brainless'. This is by far the best approach, and anyone familiar with political messaging on Facebook, TikTok or the Platform Formerly Known as Twitter will know that political posts quite often have nothing to do with the party or the politician they're somehow boosting. Much of this 'messaging' is nothing of the sort. There IS no message. There is only curiosity, and the impulse to share your curiosity, disdain or bewilderment.

And of all these the greatest is bewilderment. What your social media strategy team will deliver is garish nonsense with traction. Here are just a few recent viral memes devised by teams free to ignore political purpose and focus on the WTF factor:

The message: We're investing more than ever in the NHS.

The message: We will look at restructuring the Home Office to make asylum processing more efficient.

The message: We will ensure that Britain's economy becomes the most successful transformative powerhouse in world history.

Otters line-dancing on the moon to a country and western song, but it's just the name of the politician over and over again.

A weird guy in a top hat riding a unicycle through the Healing Fields at Glastonbury, scattering handfuls of granola and shouting 'Top show, what what!' at everyone.

Toddlers excitedly playing in a paddling pool.

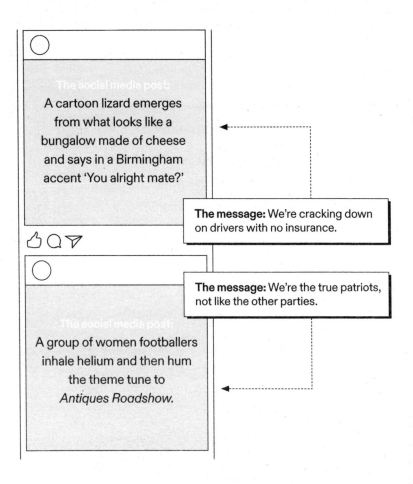

The social media post:
A cartoon lizard emerges from what looks like a bungalow made of cheese and says in a Birmingham accent 'You alright mate?'

The message: We're cracking down on drivers with no insurance.

The message: We're the true patriots, not like the other parties.

The social media post:
A group of women footballers inhale helium and then hum the theme tune to *Antiques Roadshow*.

It's pointless trying to work out what any of it means unless you're between eighteen and twenty-two years old. Just accept that this university-age demographic can tilt things firmly your way. They've got enough on their plate, what with debt before they even start a career, unaffordable rents and a ridiculous world apparently on its last legs thanks to the cheerful mismanagement by coal-burning boomers. Let them have their nonsense.

'Supermac' took over from Eden in 1957 when Elvis was at his peak, and resigned just as the Beatles made it big in 1963. His term spanned a period of affluence – 'Never had it so good' – sailing into the 1960s on 'winds of change'. He had contempt for politicians who had not seen military service, and packed 35 government posts with Old Etonians, treating them as junior officers on a battlefield.

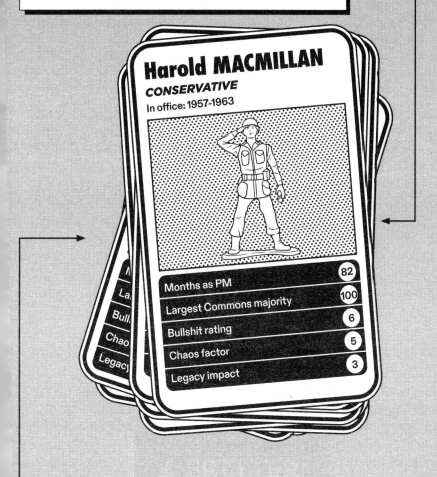

Harold MACMILLAN
CONSERVATIVE
In office: 1957-1963

Months as PM	82
Largest Commons majority	100
Bullshit rating	6
Chaos factor	5
Legacy impact	3

Sex and spy scandals piled up and he began to be seen as emblematic of establishment decay; he panicked, sacked six Cabinet ministers in his own Night of the Long Knives; that didn't help, he got ill - and resigned. Vibe: armed landowner.

Take the Slog Out of Slogan

The slogan. It needs to sound as though you mean it, but be meaningless enough to believe in. Here is the Ultimate Slogan Generating Matrix, from which even the most unimaginative campaign team can assemble a killer slogan. Just bang together the words below to make an empty yet compelling slogan. Good luck!

A	GIVE	WITH	NEW
THE	FOR	NOT	BACK
STRONG	HOPE	CAN	IS
FUTURE	BEFORE	CONTROL	CHANGE
BRITAIN	BECAUSE	TAKE	BELIEVE
BETTER	PEOPLE	STABILITY	IN
OUR	FAIRER	STRIVE	VOTE
AIM	GOOD	FORWARD	FAIR
TOGETHER	MAKE	LET'S	BE
GO	SHARE	US	YOU
WE	NATIONAL	POWER	SHOULD
CHILDREN	PROTECT	LIVE	FREE
BEST	BRIGHTER	ONE	INTO
GET	WIN	GREAT	WORLD

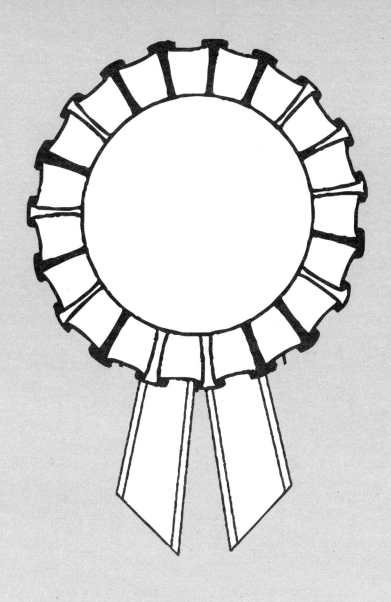

Commas, exclamation marks, etc. at user's discretion.
All words may be used more than once in a slogan,
e.g. FOR A BRIGHTER FUTURE, AND
BRIGHTER CHILDREN.

Sound Off

Once an election has been called – by you if you're in government, by your enemies if you're not – everything changes. Suddenly – as long as your team don't want to make you super-boring (see above) – you're required to present yourself as resolute, confident and combative.

That's why, whether you like it or not, you will be assigned an 'attitude coach'. Because every election campaign must these days be momentumised by a barking American who can say words such as 'momentumised' with a straight face. It means subjecting you and your team to withering, humiliating trust exercises, physical challenges and debate rehearsals.

Be prepared for the sheer volume of insults coming your way, too. The template for every attitude coach is the drill sergeant from Stanley Kubrick's *Full Metal Jacket*. Potential prime ministers would be well advised to watch this so they don't get a shock when the tough times begin. Exercises will start with you and your colleagues standing up straight in a line while the attitude coach prowls past you all with a mad look in his eyes. He doesn't care what sex you are, either. Just because men cry more easily during these humiliations doesn't mean he'll ease up on the lads. After half an hour or so of character assassination in the foulest language imaginable, it'll be time for the Talking Tough Exercises. Basically, you'll be coached to respond positively to an interviewer's question with a loud 'You bet!'

This is **STAGE ONE**, which will soon escalate through gradations of vulgar assertiveness:

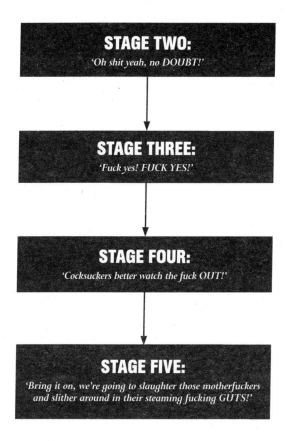

STAGE TWO:
'Oh shit yeah, no DOUBT!'

STAGE THREE:
'Fuck yes! FUCK YES!'

STAGE FOUR:
'Cocksuckers better watch the fuck OUT!'

STAGE FIVE:
'Bring it on, we're going to slaughter those motherfuckers and slither around in their steaming fucking GUTS!'

[Note: Recommended up to Stage Three only for *Newsnight*.]

PM Interview Bingo

If you can slip most of these tiny slivers of deflective, playing-for-time bullshit into a five-minute interview, you're golden. You can practise by watching the prime minister bluff and block their way through a TV interview or, if you're feeling very very patient, listen to the *Today* programme on Radio 4.

★ B ★ I ★ N ★ G ★ O ★

I'm sorry, that's not my understanding	That's not a reality I recognise	I have been very clear about this	Britain deserves the truth
Please, let me finish	You're really asking the wrong question	Look, I'm not going to play games	Listen, I want to be honest with you here
Let me answer your first question, if I may	That's not what we're hearing on the doorstep	Sorry, I don't quite understand what you're asking	This is not about me. This is about what's best for the country
Ha ha ha, no I'm not falling into that trap	Look, I was invited here to talk about [X], not this	That's not the view of the backbenchers I've spoken to	I have been clear, this government will deliver on its promises

Surprise appointment (everyone expected Rab Butler to be PM) in 1963, just in time for the JFK assassination and a terrible relationship with President Lyndon Johnson after the sale of British Leyland buses to Cuba.

Alec DOUGLAS-HOME
CONSERVATIVE
In office: 1963-1964

Months as PM	12
Largest Commons majority	100
Bullshit rating	7
Chaos factor	2
Legacy impact	2

He lasted a year. Macmillan described him as 'steel painted as wood'. Derided by the posh, smart-arse new generation of satirists as out of touch and aristocratic. Vibe: plastinated corpse.

We're H A P P B

Party Political Broadcasts (PPBs). They're traditional, of course, which is the problem. Everybody knows why you want to do it: you love the idea of looking like a political figurehead. But what about viewers?

On the one hand, nobody wants to see you clogging up their viewing time. On the other, nobody wants to hear you either. PPBs are traditional in the same way as the monarch's speech on Christmas Day is: old-fashioned, creaking under the weight of its own lost cultural luggage, boring as hell. You should give serious consideration to letting your meme team, their enthusiasm undimmed by months of social media larks, have a go. Imagine what they might unleash for a five-minute slot.

Because if you seriously think five minutes of you sitting at a desk talking calmly about your policy agenda in what looks like a corner of Clement Attlee's study will get the vote out, then congratulations: you're well on track to win the 1951 general election. Meanwhile, back in the now world, viewers are processing barrages of saturated colour and high-volume, compressed, x2-speed shouting coming from several directions at once. A politician sitting in a chair for five minutes isn't going to keep people watching, unless someone's set fire to the desk and you're trying to front it out. You need fresh thinking.

Why not try podcasts hosted by shitposters? These people don't want to humiliate you like those nasty TV journalists, they just want you to be entertaining. Can you yodel? Recite pi to the 100th decimal place? Rank animals by attractiveness? Or you could make the PPB an anthology: here's what I've been up to recently. And it's just a series of ten or so thirty-second clips featuring an augmented version of you petting a dog or scoring a goal or lip-syncing to a clip of your political nemesis sounding stupid – plus, boom, you're dressed as a clown. The possibilities, unfortunately, are limitless. Choose wisely, but always follow the advice of someone no older than half your age.

CHAPTER 6:
MONEY

People these days have all sorts of outgoings, things are getting more expensive, everyone's on a tight budget. How much extra do you think the average consumer would pay for politics? Ha ha, yeah exactly. People can already get hours and hours of dramatised corruption and backstabbing on all of the main streamers AND terrestrial telly. And let's face it: fictional politicians are a lot more attractive on TV than the real ones, who always have that shifty look, that feigned innocence of the teenager who absolutely has not been smoking weed. Don't worry, you won't look like that. (see Chapter 7).

It costs a fortune to keep a political party going, and even more to bankroll an election campaign. Where does the money come from? Donations and bequests, fundraising appeals, mysterious loans, gifts in kind. Financial resources for driving your triumphant ascent to PM can come from many directions, in many guises and, if your donors have shrewd financial advisers, many disguises too. Your ethical judgement here really determines what you will and won't accept, as an honourable person.

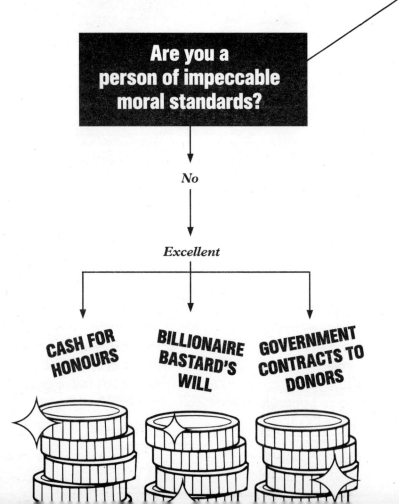

Are you a person of impeccable moral standards?

No

Excellent

CASH FOR HONOURS

BILLIONAIRE BASTARD'S WILL

GOVERNMENT CONTRACTS TO DONORS

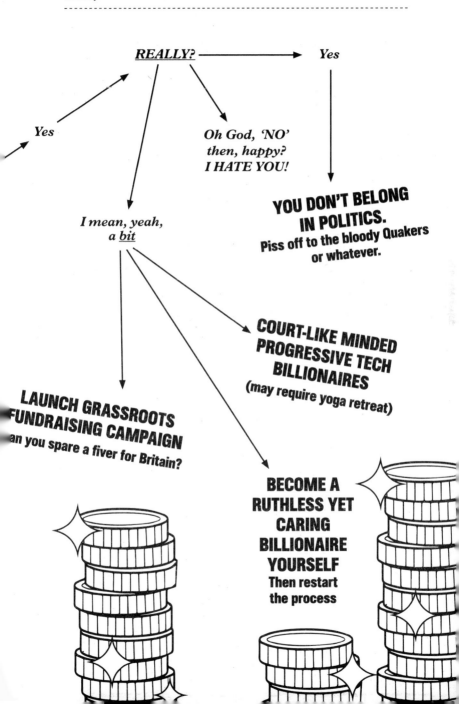

A Run for Their Money

What sort of donee are you? And yeah, that is a word. Donors need to be charmed, so find a way to be charming that plays to your personality type, and strengths. And to theirs. Find your extremely rich soulmate and watch the campaign cash come hosing in! Take a long, hard look at the type of self you are, then go for the corresponding type of selves the donors are, and ker-CHING!

AGREEABLE. The chief characteristics of your personality type are compassion and politeness. Your list of donor targets should include rich people with impeccable manners and a soft spot for animals. Introduce yourself formally in the first instance by sending a polite and compassionate letter praising their work in saving polar bears or whatever. You can promise that one of the first acts of your government would be to save as many polar bears as possible. Obviously, for God's sake don't promise to reverse global warming, that would be nuts. But you could pledge to open a polar bear sanctuary as a matter of priority. Arrange to meet the potential donor at one of those stuffy London clubs; they always look quite agreeable.

CONSCIENTIOUS. Your chief characteristics are industriousness and orderliness. Your list of donor targets should focus on industrialists and people with a fetish for punctuality and order. Perhaps you've got your eye on a billionaire manufacturer of clinical instruments, or of any number of precise-measurement items the NHS needs by the lorryload. Your approach should be formal and thorough. Make it clear that you respect 'not just business but busyness' and that in your own private life you have some nerdy passion connected to orderliness that mirrors in some way your target's fussy obsession with efficiency and statistics. Pretend you are a model railway enthusiast or an amateur cricket umpire. Make your ideal donor connection through an industrious programme of research to find the right target, and then research the target's hobby. You don't actually have to be a model train obsessive or a statistician, you just have to know enough to secure a whopping donation.

EXTROVERT. Your chief characteristics are assertiveness and enthusiasm. Fortune favours the bold, so you need to pair with a target donor who shares your own gung-ho approach. Extroverts love to see in others the same slightly scary levels of enthusiasm and confidence that got them where they are today: at the top of their profession, with millions to spare for the right cause. Introduce yourself at a party with a crushing handshake and demand to know if they too used to be in the army. Even the most glancing of introductions will set you up for your main approach. Arrive unannounced and super-assertive at the donor's office, wave aside the secretary telling you they're in a meeting, burst into their office, point at everyone but your target shouting 'Right, everyone out – NOW!' Then give your target a steady look and say 'We need to talk about how much fucking money you're going to give me, yes?' It cannot fail.

OPEN TO EXPERIENCE. Your chief characteristics are openness and intellect. Your donor targets will have big brains and curious minds, so you need to step up your game here. Approaching the head of some highly successful scientific endeavour requires tact and intelligence. Perhaps your target's business operation oversees research into effective vaccines. Maybe their laboratories grow experimental meat substitutes. Your strategy team needs to do their own research. They need to wangle a guest speaker spot for you at a science conference your donor is addressing. Your own address will be an innocuous speech which nevertheless calls for substantial public sector investment in whatever it is your donor does for a living. Be very keen to meet them at the buffet lunch, and prepare in advance some targeted spiel about their field of enquiry, dropping in just enough knowledge to show you have a vague grasp but getting them to do most of the talking. Present a political donation as a Newtonian power principle: an investment in you as potential prime minister will be met with an equal investment in their expanding workload.

NEUROTIC. Your chief characteristics are volatility and withdrawal. As a neurotic, you will be desperately seeking, and then ignoring, targets who have the same disposition. You want donors who are thin-skinned, who suffer periods of extreme self-doubt, and whose mood can veer from gloomy to ecstatic in a heartbeat. Writers might seem like a good target, but the only writers who can afford a sizeable donation will be the successful ones, and they will have their self-doubt very much under control. Artists and popular music stars are your best bet, as they are extremely volatile and often a bit dim. Here, withdrawal is key. Arrange a lunch and then pull out at the last minute. Do this two or three times. Tell them you have stage fright or impostor syndrome – they'll love that. When you finally do meet, be hunched and withdrawn in dark glasses and sound depressed about the future of the popular arts. They will cough up and feel very good about themselves, and you will have made the world a better place, for them at least.

Working-class meritocrat. Yachtsman, musician, author, Europhile, bachelor. Oversaw decimalisation. Local government reform reduced the number of local authorities and created metropolitan counties. Heath led Britain's entry into the EC, the precursor of the EU. The worsening Troubles in Northern Ireland led him to introduce internment and direct rule.

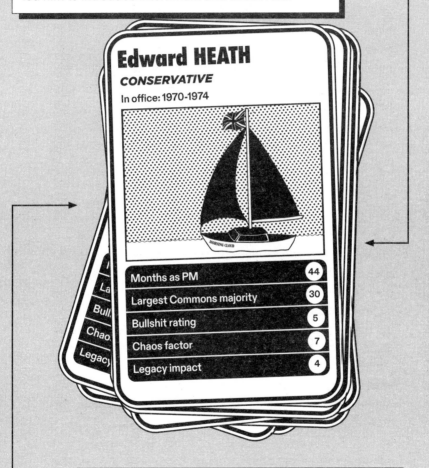

Edward HEATH
CONSERVATIVE
In office: 1970-1974

Months as PM	44
Largest Commons majority	30
Bullshit rating	5
Chaos factor	7
Legacy impact	4

Sickness and other state benefits were reduced, pensions increased. Called a general election to determine who ruled Britain, the government or the unions; got the answer he didn't want. Vibe: shifty gynaecologist.

The Most Honourable Donors

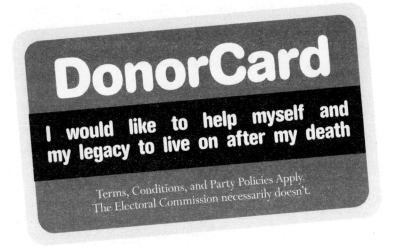

Those of a delicate disposition may find it difficult to swallow the hard, knotty bolus of 'cash for honours'. And that's why everyone, including you – especially you – is very much against the process. 'Let me be clear', you will say in an interview, 'I absolutely deplore the idea of bestowing honours in return for donations. It is not a practice I condone, and certainly not one I recognise personally from my own interactions with this country's foremost innovators and heroes, who work tirelessly towards making this country the most dynamic economy in the developed world.'

The important thing here is to separate – both in your own mind and in any possibly incriminating trail of paperwork – the two aspects of this. The honour and ~~the bribe~~ donation. An example: that buccaneering arsehole who runs a business specialising in government software and maintenance contracts. He gave ten million quid to your party because he believes in the future Britain that you and your colleagues have set out, and he'd very much like to contribute to that. That's fair enough, it's very much a free country, thanks in no small part to buccaneering arseholes very much like him. His subsequent knighthood was awarded for his extremely important work making software and governmental partnership a key driver of operational synergy across the industry and throughout cross-departmental disciplines, honestly this stuff just writes itself.

The cost of giving

Every now and then, some cynic will bewail the corruption inherent in Britain's honours system. How tawdry they find the ten million quid-pro-quo of it all, how it cheapens politics. Well, let me tell you, bewailing cynic, politics isn't getting any cheaper. Maybe it's time to update the current going rates for honours. To make the whole enterprise as transparent as possible, the exchange rates these days are arranged in tiers, like the subscription levels of crowdfunded books. Self-publishing companies offer everything from the basic book (£20), through signed copies (£25), all the way up to a deluxe edition book with handwritten bespoke sonnet and lunch with the author in a European capital of your choice (£95,000). Exactly the same principle operates in the honours racket. It's only a scandal if you can't afford it.

There was a reaction to a general sense of 'sleaze' in 1990s politics in the form of the Political Parties, Elections and Referendums Act 2000. This requires British political parties to disclose the source of all donations and loans over £7,500 to the Electoral Commission.

Obviously seven and a half grand is not going to get a donor more than a basic thank-you email from the party chairman. The rewards only really begin at a higher donation level, as follows:

£20K

Signed thank-you letter from the PM, invitation to the local party's prosecco and nibbles get-together in a Methodist church.

The above, plus selfie with PM at party conference.

£50K

£100K

The above, plus Christmas drinks at 10 Downing Street.

The above, plus your name on the next hospital children's ward to be built, subject to that actually happening.

£250K

£500K

Plus the PM will visit your place of work for fifteen minutes as an exemplar of The Britain We All Want To Live And Work In. News agencies to be alerted.

All that, plus an OBE.

All that, plus a CBE, a branded goodie bag and the PM will refer to you by your first name throughout the interaction.

The aforementioned, plus an invitation for you and a plus-one to play three rounds of pickle ball in the Number 10 garden with the PM and Chancellor of the Exchequer, along with a guarantee that you will win at least one round, a memento video, as much calamari and Cava as you can manage, plus a cab ride home (within the M25 area).

A bundled package of the above, plus knighthood.

The Platinum Knighthood Package, including your appointment as Minister Without Portfolio.

Charity begins at home

Once again, if you're starting your political journey, it might be a good idea to rehearse the notion of cash for honours – the political science of 'tit for tat' –with family members. If you have children, perfect. Kids have an innate knack for bargaining that, to a large extent, adults have lost or mislaid.

It's even possible to devise a domestic version of Cash for Honours to make the whole process understandable, transparent and not at all morally dubious. Parents are the donors and children are the slightly over-promising politicians. Encourage them to approach you with policies to improve the world (of your home) and to negotiate a sensible donation to their campaign (of earning money).

POLITICAL ACTION ➡	CASH FOR ACTION
Tidy room	£3
Tidy room + vacuum carpet	£5
Wash car	£7
Mow lawn	£10
Order of Behavioural Excellence (OBE)	£15 for weekend
Consistent Behavioural Excellence (CBE)	£20 Mon–Fri

Politics as a Game

Something else that trains you, the proto-PM, in the early days before your career starts, is politicising board games. It's more or less the ordinary bad-tempered rough-and-tumble of family fun, but even more worthwhile.

If you're playing a board game, pretend that family members are political opponents, which in many ways, of course, they are. Then even a game of snakes and ladders becomes a race to the top. A big donation speeds you on your way, a damaging sex scandal sends you down the slippery slope. Of course, if you're playing with young children they might not understand what a sex scandal is, so maybe sliding down the snake is because you got drunk and started a fight in the House of Commons.

Likewise, a game of Monopoly can easily be converted into a general election campaign – but be careful not to start one of those rolling extended-family Christmas rows. It's fine for you to say in your best Dimbleby voice: 'We're hearing that Gran has landed on Park Lane. No surprise, of course, that constituency has been staunchly blue since records began, and— oh, we're now hearing that Mayfair may have swung to Gran too. The constituency was up for grabs in the No Overall Control pile and Gran may have taken it. Yes. Confirmation there, Mayfair and Park Lane have both now swung to Gran...' You might think of the Strand and Fleet Street as red wall constituencies; they might change hands quite often, depending on economic circumstances.

But for God's sake, don't sermonise when someone buys any of the utilities once owned and run by the public sector, or bits of the once-nationalised railway. Just because your sister has bought Water Works is no excuse for calling her a 'capitalist vulture'. Nor should you launch into a diatribe about how we'll see what happens now, shall we, when a public utility once beholden to taxpayers is privatised, run as a monopoly and driven into the ground, with raw sewage pumped more or less continuously into our seas and rivers, and all wealth transferred to shareholders and hedge funds with no accountability whatsoever to consumers, who face steepling charges and have no recourse but armed revolution. Yeah thanks 'Jeremy Corbyn' for ruining Christmas. Again.

Cash for Considerations

There are, of course, options for the keen donor who is less interested in acquiring a title and more interested in legislation that might coincidentally help their business interests. Someone prominent in, say, the gambling industry might fancy a punt on your administration's sensible approach to regulating gambling. For an unsolicited sum they might be usefully asked, as an industry expert, to coordinate a government review into the regulation of the gambling industry, specifically which key areas might be left alone for the industry itself to deal with.

Party cash donors are essential in a general election year; campaigns are getting more expensive. This is partly because all kinds of stuff, from leaflets to advertising space on Facebook, costs more, and partly because parties are desperate to spend the maximum allowed, which keeps going up. In 2022 the Conservative government raised spending limits for general elections from £19m to £34m, presumably as part of its levelling-up agenda. Nature abhors a vacuum, and so does every party treasurer. Spending capacity, after all, is there to be fully capacitised.

Invisibilised Money

There are times when even the most trustworthy of donors wants to be discreet. Quite often this is because they are very modest and hate making a fuss, or showing off about how much money they have. They deserve every accommodation.

Gifts

There are ways around the cash limits, of course. We live in a pluralistic democracy and there are all sorts of people willing to help. It's possible for donors to make gifts 'in kind' that don't show up as straight money donations: helicopter rides, secretarial assistance, administration services, catering help, assistance in spa services, use of holiday home and personal railway, access to all the sorts of treats that friends routinely give one another.

Channelling money

There's also the frowned-upon (yeah, by your enemies) practice of channelling money through unincorporated associations to disguise the source. Some especially generous and newly-ennobled benefactors may have split their donations between multiple family members and businesses, and that's often a nightmare to untangle. Others may choose to pour money into think-tanks and campaigning groups with a close working relationship to your party. In an age where politics is not just vitally important but horrendously expensive, the average hard-working prime minister must be prepared to accept help from whichever direction it flows, however circuitous the route. The idea of having unrealised spending power is as unthinkable as, say, allowing child poverty to increase on your watch, or presiding over a calamitous rise in avoidable deaths because of ambulance delays.

Death

Ah yes, death. Inevitable, eventually, for all of us. Bad news for those on their way out, good news for those on their way up. It would certainly be worth your while, as a party leader aiming to become PM, to court the dying as well as the living. That sounds a bit brutal, but in 2023 a certain supermarket tycoon left the Tories £10m in his will. That's a nice bung, wherever it's come from. And the advantage of the donor being dead is that they can't embarrass you after the money's been transferred. You know what it's like: your political enemies, alert for any opportunity to shame you, will notice that someone still alive has gifted a hefty whack your way and then muckrake their way to some damning revelation. Oh, the donor's been caught on tape saying that fascism doesn't deserve the knee-jerk reaction it always seems to provoke among do-gooders and actually Hitler had some cracking ideas about discipline in schools.

Donations from the pre-deceased fall broadly into two categories: small donations, and bloody great big ones. There is no harm, or as yet any legal impediment, to your canvassing the nationwide constituency of care home residents (the secretary for health and social care should be able to get you a list). Even if only 25,000 residents coughed up a tenner each, that's a quarter of a million, and literally 0 per cent of those guys are going to make Downing Street Christmas drinks.

Took over when Wilson resigned in 1976. On the first day he was in office the government lost its majority.

James CALLAGHAN
LABOUR
In office: 1976-1979

Months as PM	37
Largest Commons majority	3
Bullshit rating	7
Chaos factor	7
Legacy impact	2

Had to rely on pacts with the Liberals and the Scottish National Party to limp on, but was finished off by the Winter of Discontent, when a wave of public-sector strikes (cue archive film of rubbish bags piled high in Leicester Square) led to an Opposition motion of no confidence. He lost: 311 votes to 310. Vibe: moany uncle.

Death-fundraising, though, is primarily about landing the fading whales, the big donors on limited time who could make a real difference to the world by leaving the political party you lead a bid wodge of money. There are bespoke, elite and extremely discreet introductory services available to party fundraisers. These work like high-class dating agencies, but they all have names such as Ghoulmates and Dying To Meet You. For a 10 per cent cut, they will introduce the terminally ill and grotesquely rich to people like you and your party treasurer. A recent innovation is to offer a legacy in the form of 'named policies' so that the benefactor may live on (for a while at least) as a Bill progresses through both Houses of Parliament, for example The Prevention of Illegal Migration to Britain Sponsored by Sir Nathan Flatley Bill. There's a whole world of scope opening up – don't shun it.

CHAPTER 7:
RE-IMAGINEERING YOU

Once you become a prominent politician (fingers crossed!), the scrutiny really starts. Scrutiny not of anything important – your principles, morals and values will be of interest only in the event of any suggestion of hypocrisy – but of your face. It helps if you're starting from a baseline this side of repugnant, but rest assured that your media training team will work miracles.

Your core team will typically include an attitude coach (think butch guy in army fatigues who looks like he could punch out a bear); a voice coach to teach you to sound even more like you by not sounding like you at all; a stance and locomotion coach who will teach you how to stand and walk properly, and treat you like the adult toddler you truly are; a demeanour coach who will train you to believe that you're telling the truth, even when you know you're not.

If you're keen to get yourself into political shape ahead of actually having a political career, get friends and family to help out, or hire cheap advice. Start emulating the easy, plausible cadence of politicians on TV – you can learn a lot by just listening to what an expensive demeanour coach's successes sound like! For standing and walking training, which to be honest is mostly about posture and confidence, why not join the Territorial Army for a few months?

There are many components to the totality of Prime Ministerial You. And of all these, the most important, of course, is the face.

Resting Pitch Face

All prime ministers have a resting face – the one that's not switched on for the media – and it's important to make yours look interesting and engaged. You're aiming for something media advisers call resting pitch face, a look that says 'Okay, I'm off-duty but my mind is active in a never-ending quest for new ideas to formulate.' Resting pitch face is incredibly important in the tiny yet highly competitive world of prime ministerial facialistics. Why? Well... here are the switched-on media faces of just some of the occupants of Number 10 from the last half-century. See if you can guess the prime ministers. It's not as easy as you think.

- ★ compassionate, professional, hardworking
- ★ visionary gaze extending beyond policy horizons
- ★ affable, self-deprecating, effortlessly clever
- ★ focused on the nuts and bolts of government
- ★ working to find ways to accommodate all factions

★ calmly resolute in every crisis
★ determined to start a new epoch of British enterprise
★ strong, self-confident and fiercely patriotic

And here are those same PMs, defined by their resting pitch faces:

★ exhausted to the point of neurological arrest
★ engaged in existential struggle with own moral vacuum
★ fat, lazy, hungover, dehydrated
★ drained of any interest in humanity unless it's good news
★ so bitter and angry it's actually changing the shape of the skull beneath the skin
★ insatiable yet dysfunctional
★ meta-ironic, as if experiencing an out-of-body sensation
★ mentally unstable, capriciously spiteful

New-Faced Two-Faced You

A prime minister will need more than one face to be successful. That's why a face coach should be an essential member of any prime ministerial media management team. They'll show you how to train your facial muscles to act as a team. A team that follows instructions. After a month of intensive face drill, your resting pitch face will be full of quiet integrity. Specific techniques include:

★ **Eyebrow Statesmanship.** You'll learn how to train your brows into knotted determination, even while asleep. You will also master 'furrowing' and individual eyebrow-arching for those moments of quiet scepticism.
★ **Jaw Tightening.** Reverse-impulse clenching will make you look like someone who could be a benevolent dictator if they wanted, but who'd much rather be a greatly loved British prime minister.

★ **Mouth Curation.** Learn how to be at rest with your mouth firmly shut. No more mouth-breathing wobble! You can even step your mouth-work up a gear with the 'semi-pout' and the 'silent whistle'.

★ **Jowl Uptake.** In politics, all sag is a drag. Fact: jowls can go up as well as down.

★ **Bag Recusal.** Eyebags are fine, if nobody's looking at you! But stowing your bags inside your face is a game-changer for all serious political players.

★ **Sweat Abatement.** Controlling sheen should never be out-sourced to a make-up department. Control your ducts, and say goodbye to 'spamface'.

★ **General Countenance Deportment.** Putting everything together for a perfectly composed face. All the elements working in harmony – just like internal party politics!

It would do you no harm at all to practise these techniques at home. First in a mirror and then, perhaps, when you feel ready, in front of family members or friends, who could mark you out of ten. Here's a handy scoresheet for them on the opposite page, with guidance notes.

Eyebrows: were the pretend PM's eyebrows working in harmony, or at odds? Did they look clear-sighted or baffled? **/10**

Jaw: Did they hold the clench, or did they keep releasing and re-clenching their jaw, like a shit ventriloquist? **/10**

Mouth: Was their clear definition in the modes? Did they look like a camp character from a 1960s Carry On film? **/10**

Jowls: Present or absent? Deduct marks if only one jowl retracted. **/10**

Eye-Bags: Same. Did the haemorrhoid cream work? **/10**

Sweat: Presentable or lamentable? There's a fine line between the sheen of a passionate orator and the flop-sweat of a gibbering berk. **/10**

Whole thing: Did they look like a credible future leader? Or just an underwhelming estate agent trying to sell a terrible house over-valued by, like, 80 per cent? **/10**

/70

Yes, You're Standing for Prime Minister

Facial confidence is just one weapon in a prime minister's armoury of pretence. The ultimate objective is to present you as a person entirely in control of the moment, and one of the most immediate ways to signal control is with your stance. Not your actual political stance on anything, obviously. Hardly anyone's interested in your position on trade deals with Venezuela, or green bonds, or civil service reform. They're looking at your actual stance. The way you stand shows the country what you stand for. The look you're going for is strong, stable and governmental.

For a lot of your time as prime minister, people will see you on a stage somewhere, shrunk to the size of their telly. It doesn't matter whether you're in the Hammersmith Apollo or that weird little press room in Westminster. And for a surprising amount of time, it doesn't matter a great deal what you say. In every TV news bulletin it will be 'the prime minister today laid out plans for...' over coverage of you walking across the stage to the lectern. Or, if you're going full California TED Talk, to the empty space in the middle of the stage.

There are three distinct stages to your assembled stance: the Entrance, the Settling and the Stand.

The Entrance

Are you going for authority or relatability? Because there's a massive gap between them.

Authority: Think carefully about your walk-on music. Not necessarily 'Ride of the Valkyries', but not necessarily not that.

You want people to fear you just the tiniest little bit. A leader, certainly. But someone whose nickname might plausibly be The Punisher, or Bitch Boss. You will stride on to that stage knowing that you own the space, and the television, and everyone watching, and the country. There will be just a hint of cruelty in the way you barely acknowledge the applause. By the time you reach your destination you will have everyone's full attention, because something about the look in your eyes and that cricket ball on the little table next to you suggests that your reaction to anyone talking at the back promises to be swift and harsh. This extreme of authoritative entrance, it should be said, is only really advisable if you've just unilaterally prorogued Parliament and declared martial law. If you're not intending to be that prime minister, dial it down.

Relatability: At the other extreme is the 'one of us' entrance. You, the prime minister, enter stage left or right, depending on your political disposition. Between your appearance and your sweet-spot arrival, you must somehow demonstrate to everyone that you're just a person, like those watching at home. This can be achieved in several ways. You could look slightly abashed, as if you don't deserve the applause, waving a little diffidently to the audience and looking as though you're the luckiest person on earth to be entrusted with this great office of state. This is okay in moderation, but you don't want to undersell your status as leader of the nation.

Talking the Walk: A warning from history – if you're having walk-on music played in, and if that music is popular or at least well-known, on no account should you make your way across the stage dancing to it. Theresa May's jaunty little 'Auntie after two sherries' bop across the stage to Abba's 'Dancing Queen' was *the most successful stage entrance dance in* *political history.* Yeah, consider that for a moment. It should sound a warning to any potential prime minister. Politicians can't dance. In recent years we have watched in horror Michael Gove's high-energy flailing, resembling a squirrel trying desperately to escape an oiled bucket. We have turned away from the unbearable spectacle of Boris Johnson wheeling and bellowing like a drowning ox to Neil Diamond's 'Sweet Caroline'. Enough. As a model modern prime minister, your dancing days are behind you, if indeed they were ever in front of you.

The successful prime minister will find a happy entrance medium, somewhere between unhinged dictator and pissed party animal. Something informal as walk-on music but not low-brow. Patriotic but this side of fascistic, maybe. Ralph Vaughan Williams, say. And an open, friendly look, as if you don't need to subdue the crowd with machine-gun fire. You're inviting people into your vision for Britain, but not in a creepy, culty way.

First female PM and longest-serving for over 150 years. Her nickname – 'The Iron Lady', given to her by a Soviet journalist – stuck. Crushed the unions, crushed Argentina in the Falklands War, crushed Britain's post-war settlement. Embraced Reaganomics, pushed through a radical programme of privatisation, introducing the notion of 'the market' to health and education sectors.

Margaret THATCHER

CONSERVATIVE

In office: 1979-1990

Months as PM	139
Largest Commons majority	144
Bullshit rating	4
Chaos factor	8
Legacy impact	10

Two Big Bangs: deregulation of the stock market and the IRA bombing of a Brighton hotel during the party conference of 1984. The miners' strike highlighted her authoritarian and combative character, with the militarisation of police forces and the outlawing of flying pickets. The Berlin Wall came down a year before Thatcher was bounced out, after polls showed she was becoming much less popular than her government. She resigned after challenges to her leadership and left feeling betrayed in 1990. Vibe: Dignitas receptionist.

Top 10 Walk-On Songs

It's never too early to practise walking on to a stage as an adored prime minister to the cheers and applause of an enthusiastic crowd of loyal party members. Here are the best walk-on tracks, as devised by the Royal Society of Ambulatory Science. Choose the one that best fits your style, get a patient family member or friend to cue the music, then enter the living room boldly, looking important, but remember – NO DANCING, not even little dancey arm movements, you'll look like a complete pillock. Ready? Let's walk on!

1. THESE BOOTS ARE MADE FOR WALKIN'
2. WALK THIS WAY
3. DO YA THINK I'M SEXY?
4. THE IMPERIAL MARCH (DARTH VADER'S THEME)
5. HERE COME THE HOTSTEPPER
6. NELLIE THE ELEPHANT
7. FIRESTARTER
8. LOVE ME DO
9. CHEEKY SONG (TOUCH MY BUM)
10. ANDANTE FROM SHOSTAKOVICH'S PIANO CONCERTO NO. 2

Oversaw Britain's longest period of continuous economic growth and the beginning of a Northern Ireland peace process. Had a pivotal role in the Good Friday agreement and the Black Wednesday fiasco.

John MAJOR

CONSERVATIVE

In office: 1990-1997

Months as PM	77
Largest Commons majority	21
Bullshit rating	6
Chaos factor	7
Legacy impact	4

A collapsing pound was withdrawn from the European Exchange Rate Mechanism, Chancellor Norman Lamont sought to prop up the currency with the help of the Bank of England, the markets crashed, interest rates soared to 15 per cent and the Tories' reputation for sound economic management drove off a cliff. Accumulating sleaze revelations in the middle of a moral crusade ('Back to Basics') and a string of by-election defeats paved the way for electoral disaster in 1997. Vibe: community policeman.

The Settling

The next stage of your composite stance. This is often overlooked by amateur politicians but is a key transitional stage. If you're heading for a lectern, bring a sheaf of notes on to the stage with you – this will make you look diligent, as though you're taking the audience so seriously that you've been working on this speech right up until showtime. Then you can casually shuffle papers at the lectern, limbering up: here I go, this is going to be brilliant. A moment of sharply focused introspection and you're settled, ready to begin.

If you're heading to the spotlight in the middle of an empty stage, you'll be entering hands-free, wearing one of those little call-centre microphones. This signals to your audience that you're relaxed enough to wing this without notes and that you're confident enough to prowl the stage like some political panther, casting your gaze here and there, an inclusive and inspirational speaker. Acknowledge the applause, humbly, and gently signal to everyone to calm down – hey, I'm just the prime minister. Then subtly change the expression on your face from warm likeability to serious player, and begin.

The Stand

Now this is, quite rightly, one of the most talked-about aspects of prime ministerial presentation and, like your policies and rhetoric, is subject to fashion. There was a fad during the 2010s for politicians to stand in a 'power pose' as if they were making cameo appearances in the Marvel Comic Universe: legs preposterously far apart, big smile, arms loose. This worked better for men in trousers than for women in skirts, but was universally adopted as the way to look transcendentally in charge. It got to the point where it was a competitive sport, with each new Cabinet member standing with their legs an extra inch apart to show that he/she was not just a team player but a team champion. Then it slowly dawned on everyone that maybe having the new home secretary standing like Little Richard didn't look impressive at all, it looked really fucking weird.

You need to look as natural as it is possible for anyone to look, alone on stage and addressing an invisible audience. If you're at the lectern, make sure it's at the right height for you to be able to grab it now and then, to subtly indicate that you've got a firm grip on things. But make sure the autocue is high enough to make you look tall and powerful. You need to stand as if you're at home, chillaxing at your kitchen island with the new Four Tet album on, chatting and joking with a few friends, but at the same time preparing an incredibly difficult and complex endive salad. The audience needs to know that you're engaged in vital work, but that there's also always time for friends.

If you're going full TED, be aware that 100 per cent of you will be visible, unobscured by lectern or anything else. You will be on the move, so watch your posture. Nobody's expecting gymnastics – you're the prime minister, not a pentathlete – but if you're putting yourself in this exposed situation to start with, you can't afford to shamble around the stage like a wounded heifer. Take small, considered movements from spot to spot, covering the stage in an unhurried way, light on your feet, balanced by firm but gentle hand-shapes in the air.

Take your pick from:

- ★ The Modest Eureka
- ★ The Thought Just Occurred
- ★ The Nothing In My Hands
- ★ The Downward Slice
- ★ The Elevated Shutter
- ★ The Magic Trick
- ★ The Self-Owning Rock-Paper-Scissors Winner
- ★ The Who Knew
- ★ The I Happily Surrender
- ★ The You're Brilliant
- ★ The Tiniest Violin
- ★ The One True God
- ★ The Two True Gods
- ★ The Ant Examination
- ★ The Swingometer
- ★ The Murmuring Heart
- ★ The Precise Chalkmark
- ★ The Mid-Air Origami
- ★ The No More For Me, I'm Driving
- ★ The Thermostat Adjustment
- ★ The Venus Fly-Trap
- ★ The Could I Have The Cheque Please
- ★ The Anglican Hand Clasp
- ★ The Wait I've Forgotten Something
- ★ The Shakespearean Fait Accompli
- ★ The Why You
- ★ The Exasperated Genius
- ★ The Musketeer Blade-swish
- ★ The Microsurgery
- ★ The Wait, What
- ★ The Stop

Labour, New version. Youngest PM of the twentieth century, longest-serving Labour PM, won Labour's largest ever general election victory. Led the nation in mourning Diana, Princess of Wales, impressing with his statesmanlike empathy. Turbo-charged the Private Finance Initiative as a showcase for public–private investment in public buildings and infrastructure. Sure Start centres set up. Minimum wage established. Civil partnerships, LGBT rights championed. Doubled spending on NHS by 2001. Invited Britpop into Downing Street as a prosperous Britain celebrated its Cool Britannia alter ego.

Tony BLAIR

LABOUR

In office: 1997-2007

Season's Greetings

Months as PM	121
Largest Commons majority	179
Bullshit rating	8
Chaos factor	2
Legacy impact	7

Close ally of George W. Bush after 2001 Twin Tower attacks. He split the party – and the nation – over his decision to join the invasion of Iraq and America's ill-defined War on Terror. Stood down in 2007 to allow someone else to deal with an imminent global economic crash and the waning popularity of New Labour. Haunted by Iraq, he nevertheless enjoys a very wealthy PM afterlife. Vibe: disgraced Pilates instructor.

The Smile

As mentioned earlier, this is an odd one for politicians generally, and prime ministers in particular, as it tends to make them all look even less trustworthy. In recent memory we have seen the tragedy of death in high office unfold behind the painted smile of surely the only person in Britain who couldn't see how vividly fake it was. It is a massive mistake to believe that presenting a smile in every circumstance is wise. You do not want to smile when somebody's asking you about job losses in the North-west. Or when listening to someone tell you how her gran passed away on a gurney in A&E because there was no bed available. If you have to smile at any of the above, make it a 'smiling through the grimness to show both sympathy and resolve to make things better' smile. Not an 'I can't wait to tell you about this totally amazing funny animal vid I saw on YouTube' smile. There are gradations of smile, and it's worth your while knowing which to deploy in any scenario.

The Bravely Spectral. This should be perceived as not really a smile at all, merely the tiniest hint of the smile reflex to stop yourself crying. Reserved strictly for visits to a disaster zone, or a four-point drop in the polls.

The Wry. The wry smile has been cheapened in recent years by opinion journalism. Nearly every column carries a byline picture of someone looking at you knowingly, as if they've just told you a terrible, hilarious secret. You know better, though. Reserve the wry smile for an awkward interview question you're not going to answer, or someone from the SNP laying into you in the Commons.

The Formal. This is a safe bet, and the smile most often deployed by politicians. It is neutral, non-committal and may be real or false, depending on the circumstances. Real if, for example, you're getting knighted by the king; false if, for example, you're getting shellacked by the political editor of *The Times*.

The Genuinely Happy. Don't panic, nobody expects you to actually be genuinely happy in public. This is the smile you deploy on holiday when you know you and your family are being photographed but you have to pretend not to have noticed the cameras.

The Accidentally Happy. Very dangerous territory indeed. This is the smile you're not in control of, because you are 100 per cent certain there are no media people around. You've idiotically relaxed, you've been persuaded by 'friends' to have another margarita or line of coke, or both. Your guard is down, and you've forgotten the two rules of accidental happiness in politics: one, that everyone with a smartphone is now a media photographer and two, that most embarrassing photos of politicians are leaked by their 'friends'. The main takeaway here is to avoid both happiness and friendship if you're at all serious about becoming prime minister. If in doubt about whether to smile, don't.

There are a few occasions when it's okay for a prime minister (you, remember?) to smile: you just heard a joke; you're posing for a selfie, or the Downing Street Christmas card; you just won a by-election. You get the idea. Situations where it would look mad and a bit sinister if you didn't look happy. But you must remember the obverse of that: any situation in which it would look mad and a bit sinister to smile, don't.

In May 2024 Monty Panesar, the former England bowler, announced he would be standing as a candidate for the Workers Party of Britain. He told the *Guardian* that if he ever addressed the nation as prime minister, the message on the lectern would read: Immigration Makes Britain Great.* Which, let's face it, is pretty good, but what would your lectern message be? Some suggestions below. Pick the one that best represents you. Or better still, bin them all and make up your own. You don't need to be pigeonholed, you're a one-off!

*A week later he left the party when he found out a bit more about it, but still. Good lectern work.

1. I'M IN CHARGE! with fairy lights around it.

2. A BRITTER BRITAIN in Comic Sans.

3. BRAIN + I T = BRITAIN! in gently pulsing LEDs.

4. I'M WITH STUPID → make sure the Chancellor's standing on the right side.

5. Have a complicated anagram (e.g. IMPISH RETIREMENT) that people have to solve before you've finished speaking.

6. The Lottery Numbers scrolling past.

7. I'M RESIGNING and I'M NOT RESIGNING alternately fading in and out, resolving only as you head back in to Number 10.

8. No words, just a big mouth with teeth. As you talk, it slowly smiles.

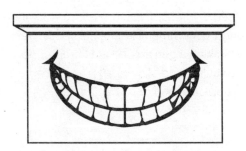

9. No words, just a slot that shoots out incense, bubbles and smoke rings.

10. As you speak, the lectern somehow rises slowly into the air with you behind it (ask some circus people or whoever to sort it out). You're giving a speech about the responsibility of the media to tell the truth. As you reach the roofline of Number 10, you finish your speech and turn the lectern down towards the press pack. The lectern slot suddenly belches harmless but terrifying Game of Thrones-alike dragon fire at them as they flee in screaming panic and you laugh like a maniac.

Dress Code

All politicians wear clothes, even in the Netherlands. But it's important to strike the right tone. You need to appear boring enough to be relatable and to at least pretend to be a team player. However, you also need to signal that you're a singular talent, someone with a strong enough personality to make their mark in politics.

You'll want to look normal, so obviously no novelty inflatable suits or outlandish costumes. You're prime minister, not part of the Village People. Dressing up in police or military gear is permissible only if you've masterminded a military coup (see A Very British COO, page 202) and even then, only for the initial televised address. People want reassurance, and to feel as though government is in safe hands. Yelling at the camera and waving a gun around are barely coded signals of instability, volatility and Americans on Facebook. This is Britain: we keep calm and don't carry guns.

For men: Suits, of course, but ties optional. Not optional everywhere, though. You can't go tieless to the funeral of a valued and much-loved political rival, or when you're giving a speech at Mansion House. If it's for a photoshoot, however, lose the tie. You'll look more human, which is the greatest trick of all in politics. However: plain ties and suits please, you're not a bloody children's entertainer.

For women: Anything this side of 'reception class teacher' is broadly acceptable. There is no detail in your outfit that cannot be enlarged, pored over and mocked. That modest little brooch in your lapel, the one that innocently depicts a leaping gazelle. You've deliberately worn it, so it must mean something. Try not to give the bastard photographers any help at all. Dress as if you're the judge, in court, listening to a man trying to explain how he lost control of the car. Summary: it's a shitshow for women, in politics as everywhere else.

His stint as Chancellor became the longest period of economic growth. In 1997, took PM baton from Blair, ran straight into terrorist attacks, the Credit Crunch, a run on the banks and a major recession. With his Chancellor, Alistair Darling, he devised rescue packages for banks, but he and the Labour party increasingly looked like slowly deflating balloons.

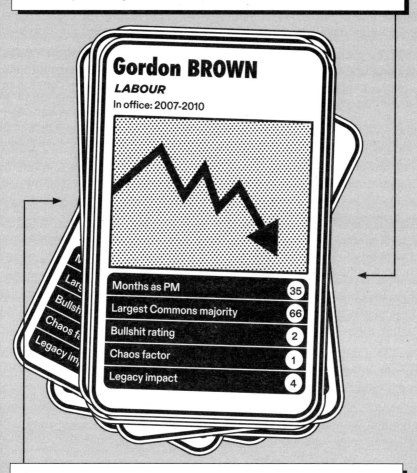

Gordon BROWN

LABOUR

In office: 2007-2010

Months as PM	35
Largest Commons majority	66
Bullshit rating	2
Chaos factor	1
Legacy impact	4

It was generally felt that he dithered, and should have called an election in 2007. The 2010 general election didn't give him a majority. Attempts to form a coalition with the Lib Dems failed and they decided to ally with the Conservatives instead. His was the first government to introduce a Climate Change Act. Vibe: human raincloud.

CHAPTER 8:
YOU AND THE INTERVIEW

Now your team has got you looking good, you need to make sure you're fighting fit. Journalism is a war, you against them, and the interview is a battleground.

Interview Training

Some minor politicians, and those at the acutely naive end of the audience spectrum, still insist that the purpose of any political interview is forensic interrogation. Whereas it's generally accepted within the media and the political world that the Big Interview is simply a form of non-physical close combat. It's not what is said, or what is revealed or omitted, that counts. It's who wins. In conventional interview combat, the interviewer will often become more aggressive as the battle wears on, the interviewee takes defensive action and uses a range of evasive techniques. Attacker versus defender.

And the UK is not the US, where there is still residual respect for the Office of President, if not for the actual incumbent. No such deference here, where the best a prime minister can hope for from journalists is a condescending mix of genial contempt and genuine pity. The official war-studies laboratory for trying out new techniques of both attack and defence is of course the flagship interview on Radio 4's *Today* programme. It's often impossible to listen to, for the reason that this form of combat gets locked quite early into stalemate. However exasperated the interviewer gets, the politician will answer only on their terms. Here are some classic moves to keep you in control.

1. The Swerve

You, the prime minister, are up for a showcase interview. It's a one-on-one fight. Radio or television, the rules are the same. At the start the interviewer is friendly and welcoming. This is a feint: the media landscape is a primeval jungle, the interviewer is a predator and you are on this breakfast show because you are the breakfast. They make an impertinent demand to know something you are 100 per cent not going to reveal. Let's say the date of the next general election. Laughing this off (NO, don't literally do that), you insist the listener wants to know instead about some fantasy plan of yours to turbo-charge Britain into the twenty-third century, by Christmas. The interviewer asks again about the election date, is again rebuffed and admonished. The British public just want to see this government get on with the very important work of blah blah and so on. Who won? A social media jury is always on hand to score the bout, which quite often is judged to be a draw. Boring and pointless.

2. The Block

There are certain prime ministerial moves which once were innovative and worked pretty well, but by now are dated and easily countered. You just refuse to answer the question. In the olden days, you might have told the interviewer the question was impertinent and that they should apologise, or else agree to a duel in Regent's Park. These days a favourite tactic is to say that you can't answer the question as there is an inquiry in progress and you will not second-guess its conclusions. Or you might say that you're unable to answer the question due to commercial sensitivities, which you can invent in advance. Just don't do the full flounce and strop off. You know why? It doesn't work. Running away from an interview is not winning, it's losing. 'You block, you're a cock,' as they all say at Broadcasting House.

3. The Different Answer

In this well-worn tactic, the prime minister, instead of answering the question they've been asked, answers another question instead. Let's see it in action:

Toby: 'Prime minister, is it true that you've asked the Treasury to assess the impact of increasing corporation tax by 3 per cent?'

Prime minister: 'Toby, yes. I am entirely focused on making sure that hard-working families are given all the help they need to prosper in what are quite challenging times financially.'

Toby: 'You mention families, but my question specifically relates to businesses. Should small businesses in this country brace themselves for a rise in corporation tax?'

Prime minister: 'As I say, my job is to make sure that working men and women are given all the support we can muster in the really quite challenging times we live through—'

Toby: 'It's a simple question. Are you planning to increase corporation tax or not?'

Prime minister: 'I'm not getting into hypotheticals, Toby. I remain focused on making sure that hard-working—'

Toby: 'We're out of time, thank you prime minister. Now, weight-loss drugs. Do they work, and will they be widely available on the NHS?'

Prime minister: 'Toby, I have set out this government's priorities. They are to—'

Toby: 'The interview is over, we're now moving on to the issue of weight-loss drugs, prime minister. Sam, can we kill this mic please?'

Yes, astonishingly that was an actual transcript.

4. The Pause and Clear

One of the most recognisable strategies for avoiding direct answers to questions is the weaponised pause. Nothing wrong-foots an interviewer more than a strange silence before answering. The longer the better. After three seconds you absolutely know the producer will be screaming into the interviewer's earpiece 'WHAT THE FUCK IS GOING ON, HAVE THEY ACTUALLY DIED? KICK THEM OR SOMETHING!'

It's worth practising this technique, as it has the element of total surprise, not to mention disquiet, and immediately hands you a weird advantage. What really hammers it home is when, after a pregnant pause, you say magisterially 'Let me be clear...' and then say something deliberately obscure. 'Prime minister, what did you tell the Israeli ambassador yesterday that apparently caused such outrage?' Wait... wait... long enough for everyone to be wondering if you've had a cardiac arrest. 'Let me be clear. The future of container shipping and its impact on the global economy is something that ought to concern anyone with an interest in humane livestock exports.' And just stop there. With a bit of luck, there'll be a reciprocal weird pause from the interviewer. Obviously, the danger is that if you use this strategy too much you'll start to seem genuinely bonkers, which might affect your public approval rating. Use sparingly.

5. The Reality Check

This is the relatively recent trick of pretending that you and the interviewer are operating in entirely different realities. Being baffled by the interviewer's actual words has become very fashionable lately. Here's an example:

Interviewer: 'Prime minister, your backbenchers are in revolt over this issue, you know they are.' Moderation here is advised. By all means say 'Well I'm sorry, Fay, but that's not a reality I recognise. I have this morning had a very productive meeting with some of those backbenchers. Politics is never going to produce a happy consensus all the time. That would be absurd. But we as I say had a fruitful meeting and all of us are determined to find a way forward together.' Good. Yes. Just don't fall into the trap of taking the alternative-universe theory too seriously. Don't say 'That is not a reality I recognise. I'm sorry, but I simply do not accept what you're saying as being grounded in any reality I recognise, even a reality adjacent to the one I do recognise, in which none of this alternate, theoretically existing, reality exists...' Bad.

6. The Soundbite Salvo

There is, of course, the straightforward 'soundbite war of attrition' approach to interview conflict. The interviewer has a target answer to bag, the prime minister has a soundbite to repeat that will, ideally, become embedded in the media consciousness for the next twelve hours. Let's take a look at it in action:

Sarah (interviewer): 'Prime minister, will you apologise to the Speaker of the Commons?'

Prime minister: 'My personal relationship with the Speaker is exactly that: personal, Sarah. Unlike my government's new and extremely public campaign called Match Up to Catch Up, which we hope will—'

Sarah: 'Before we come on to that I just want to ask if you will apologise—'

Prime minister: 'Sarah, what I will NOT apologise for is our campaign, which is called Match Up to Catch Up, a scheme that aims to partner local—'

Sarah: 'As of last night, the Speaker said he had not yet heard from your office. Will you—'

Prime minister: 'As I say, Match Up to Catch Up. Match Up to Catch Up will...'

7. The Orderly Queue

The best delaying and deflecting tactics are those where you sound reasonable. Let the interviewer ask a series of interlinked questions which might, in bad faith, be taken as separate questions:

Prime minister: 'Well, let me answer one question at a time...'

Sean (interviewer): 'The question is very simple, prime minister. Do you, or do any of your family members, own shares in the controversial surveillance software developer Psyclops Intel Incorporated?'

Prime minister: 'With respect Sean, I will take your questions in the order you presented them. Your first question was "do I take transparency in politics seriously", and I'll answer that first. Although interestingly, that too may be thought of as being a multiple question, so let me begin, if I may, at the beginning. When you use terms such as "transparency" and "politics", they may not mean the same thing to everyone watching this interview...'

And so on, until you've run the clock down.

8. Be Bold, Be New, Be You

Because these strategies and counter-strategies are now so much part of the game, it may well be worth your while devising, with your media manager, new twists on the old playbook. For instance, why not insist on answering a question the interviewer asked you three months ago when you were last on the programme, on the pretext that you're simply answering questions in sequence?

Or, if you're being interviewed remotely on live television, simply behave as if you are a correspondent for the programme. So when the reporter asks: 'Prime minister, will you sack your culture secretary for her remark that only cultural Marxists read books and that woke film directors should be jailed?' simply fiddle with your earpiece as if waiting for some improbable time delay to resolve itself, then say 'Thanks Jenny. Well, I'm here with the choir of St Dunstan's Academy, Walthamstow', (here you walk over to a school choir, forcing the camera and sound guys to follow you) 'who have turned our community mentoring scheme – Match Up to Catch Up – into a very, excuse the pun, matchy-catchy little tune! Okay kids, take it away!' They'll cut you off at some point, but not before you've both avoided an awkward question and punted your soundbite, again. This is probably something you'll want to do just once, for a laugh. More than once and you'll never be interviewed by that media operation again.

With Chancellor George Osborne and the support of Lib Dem coalition partners, he introduced austerity measures. The Health and in Social Care Act abolished primary care trusts and eased more in privatisation. The Welfare Reform Act introduced a penalty for 'under-occupancy': the controversial Bedroom Tax.

David CAMERON
CONSERVATIVE
In office: 2010-2016

Months as PM	74
Largest Commons majority	78
Bullshit rating	7
Chaos factor	8
Legacy impact	3

The Tories won the general election of 2015, then Cameron tried calling the bluff of party right-wingers who wanted to leave the EU and called a referendum in 2016 which showed a majority wanted to leave. Cameron resigned to spend more time in his luxury writing wagon. His PM afterlife involved a lobbying career and a recall, as Lord Cameron, to the foreign office. Vibe: mafia accountant.

Kitchen Politics

Home is where the artfulness is, and a domestic setting is ideal for practising interview combat techniques. Surprise your partner or children or flatmate one morning by being aggressively defensive about everything. Treat every question as a trick question.

Which of the eight interview techniques above should you try in response to the following questions? (A word of caution: your nearest and dearest may be puzzled, even angered, by your unreasonable behaviour. Good. This will prepare you for the performative exasperation of professional interviewers.)

All eight questions may be answered with one or other of the eight techniques. Have a go and see how you get on. There are no 'right' answers, although the ones below match up quite well:

A: Try Orderly Queue.

'One question at a time. You were asking earlier if I'd seen your mobile.'

'I need my PE kit, have you...'

'With respect, I'll take your questions in order. As to your mobile phone, it was on 12 per cent, I plugged it in over there, it's charging.'

'Ugh I HATE you! I'll find it myself!'

'Oh, the conversation's over, is it? By the way, I do know where your PE kit is...'

B: Try the Swerve.

'Oh, thanks for noticing I shopped yesterday, by the way. Two bloody great big bags of it, got arms like an orangutan now.'

'Right, thank you SO much for shopping yesterday. I asked if today you will finally fix...'

'Sorry, I'm going to stop you there. I remain fully committed to the timely delivery of essential supplies, and I refuse to compromise on that.'

C: Try the Pause and Clear.

[You say nothing]

> 'Too ashamed to even answer me? Did you or did you
> not... don't stick your finger in the air like a cricket
> umpire, what the fuck is the matter with you? Did you
> or did you not eat my fucking granola?'

'Let me be clear, have we got any of those posh biscuits left? Or have they been eaten?'

D: Try the Block.

'I can't answer your question at the moment as I'm still processing, and frankly I refuse to second-guess my own mind...'

E: Try the Soundbite Salvo.

'Teeth Before YouTube'

> 'But I've got loads of—'

'Teeth Before YouTube'

> 'It's not even half past!'

'Teeth Before YouTube.'

F: Try the Different Answer.

'Mmm? Yes, today I will remember to pack a lunch...'

'Tea?'

'I can see what you're trying to do, but I am entirely focused on the very real problem of a packed lunch.'

'Please yourself, I'm right by the kettle is all, I'm having one, so—'

'My focus is very much on lunch, its successful inclusion in my bag, and—'

'Oh, shove your lunchbox up your arse and make your own tea.'

G: Try the Be Bold.

[filming self] 'You join us in the kitchen, where attempts at resolving an already fraught situation have been further complicated by—'

'Final notice? Why are you so determined to turn our life into a fucking Ken Loach film?'

'It seems the fragile detente has collapsed amid recriminations and – ow! – fresh violence.'

'You know what, I'm giving you final notice!'

'More as we get it. Back to you in the studio, Jen...'

H: Try the Reality Check.

'Last week. We agreed then. I said I'd make it up to you by going to your parents' for New Year.'

'We have absolutely, 100 per cent, had no such conversation.'

'Well, I'm sorry, you must be operating in a separate reality to mine, because that's what we agreed.'

'Oh yeah, my reality apparently is quite retro these days because it's gaslit!'

'My clear understanding is that—'

'Okay, compromise. You go to your mum's, I'll stay here with some luxury ready meals, a ziggurat of wine boxes and a three-day *Grey's Anatomy* binge.'

Performance Coaching

It's such a combative atmosphere now in the media that an aspiring PM and their potential Cabinet are bound to seek the help of a professional performance coach. Preparing politicians for the kind of media onslaught they can expect when in government was once an arcane branch of PR. Now it is a rapidly expanding, and feared, niche profession. Media coaches are usually American, embittered and extremely angry. It's their job to hate you and humiliate you. It's all preparation for the day you go over the top as the new prime minister to face an army of journalists, presenters and interviewers who are themselves scrabbling for status and who want to take you down as a way of getting a reputation as a giant-killer.

However distasteful it is to be told to 'stand in the fucking corner and don't say another goddamn word until I tell you to move', it's important to do as your media coach says. Resistance could lead to physical assault, a waiver for which you signed as part of the contract. In mocked-up studios, they will rehearse you to the point of exhaustion, waiting for you to commit a messaging error, then pounce. Literally, with a fly swat in your face. And they really sting.

Your performance coach will take the role of interviewer and subject you to a series of bewildering behaviours: asking questions while flapping their 'wings' around you, pretending to be a giant predatory bird; sitting staring at you, refusing to speak, daring you to start the interview without being asked a question; firing questions at you literally every thirty seconds from a tennis-ball machine loaded with special balls with scribbled words on; holding you upside-down outside a second-floor window, giving you five seconds to answer a question or they'll let go.

You probably won't have access to a proper performance coach until you're a senior politician. Until then, ask a family member or acquaintance to bully you instead. By 'family member' of course you will correctly infer that it's someone you're probably related to by marriage or any other non-bloodline turn of events. Make sure they hate you; you will have to pay them to make the exercise real, so let's assume the feeling's mutual in the end. By 'acquaintance', of course, you will again infer that it should be an enemy.

Don't worry, it will all absolutely be worth it in the end.

Catapulted into the job after a farcical leadership race which saw Michael Gove sabotage Boris Johnson. Famous for creating a 'hostile environment' for immigrants and sending 'Go Home' vans around city streets. Her term was dominated by Brexit. With full backing of the *Daily Mail*, she called a snap election in 2017 to 'crush the saboteurs' but reduced her majority.

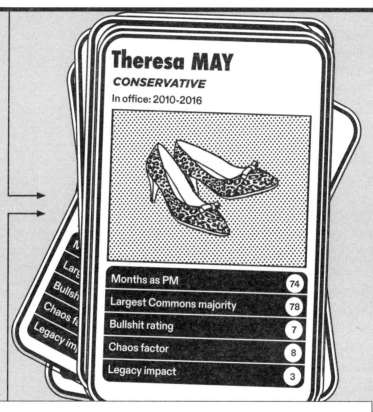

Theresa MAY

CONSERVATIVE

In office: 2010-2016

Months as PM	74
Largest Commons majority	78
Bullshit rating	7
Chaos factor	8
Legacy impact	3

She pushed on with the support of the right-wing DUP, who were ~~bribed~~ incentivised with investment schemes for a Confidence and Supply government. Terrorist attacks in London and Manchester, the Grenfell Tower fire and the Windrush scandal (people wrongly detained, denied legal rights, threatened with deportation) undermined her leadership slogan of 'strong and stable' government. She survived two votes of no confidence, but after three versions of her Brexit withdrawal agreement were defeated, she resigned in 2019, with a gentle push from the parliamentary Conservative party. Vibe: tetchy hotelier.

CHAPTER 9:
SCHMOOZING THE NEWS

Who do you most need on your side as prime minister? The obvious – and therefore wrong – answer is 'the people'. The last few years have demonstrated that a) a prime minister may be elected by a few hundred people in their party without needing to consult the public at all, and b) they may plough on in an apparently carefree way for months – months that feel like decades – with their approval ratings considerably worse than those for, say, internet scammers targeting the elderly.

Your most useful allies as a prime minister are 'the media'. Grammatically simplified in the singular, the media is in reality very plural indeed. Newspapers, magazines, online publications, social media platforms, TV, radio, podcasts: there are a million ways these days to ridicule and attack even the most blameless of prime ministers.

Your aim, as an aspiring politician, will be to charm an editor or a proprietor into swinging behind you, giving you favourable coverage in return for promises of certain policies in your legislative programme if you make it to Downing Street.

Through the Media Maze

It can be difficult, as a rising politician, to know the best route to reach your intended audience. Let's say you and your media manager have a document in your possession that may not necessarily show your party or your government in a good light, but it does make you look really bloody good. Dilemma? Exactly. The dilemma you have is deciding whether to have it leaked anonymously to a TV, radio or newspaper journalist, or just float it on social media. If you have a good relationship with a reporter, it might be worth giving them exclusive access. The quid pro quo is that they present you in a flattering light.

The same can't be said for social media platforms, which have the unified editorial stance of a bus queue. The important relationships you have in the world of print media – editors, journalists, opinion formers – simply don't exist in the same hierarchical structure on social media. They're called platforms because their defining characteristic is that of a plinth stretching out to infinity: a space filled with bitterly disappointed people with all kinds of dark and troubled thoughts. Like constituents, but actually much better because social media platforms have the power to amplify your brilliance with likes and reposts.

These days, a big story by definition has to be a trending topic on socials, however it found its way there. Let's say your plan is to leak the 'potentially quite damaging for your party but actually quite good for you' story to a contact in the print media. The advantage they'll have is that as soon as the story appears in print – perhaps even in advance of that – it will appear on the newspaper's website and social media accounts. This means that if the story's interesting it will be reposted quickly, and all the front pages of print competitors will carry it the next day, disguised as their own story. Along with all the other stories lazily culled from Facebook and the others. It's worth remembering that for newspapers, quite a lot of the 'news' coverage might just as well be called 'Yesterday On Social Media'.

The New Socialism

You may wish to cut out the middle man altogether and detonate the story on social media from the start. Newspapers will soon scoop it up anyway. Here's a quick guide to choosing the right platform.

TWITTER/X. There's always something in any story to irritate the thin-skinned lunatics who dominate here. Let a well-known political poster leak it, but make sure they make a fatal grammatical error that'll mobilise the pedants and increase clickthrough. And ideally, find an angle that you can link vaguely to 'free speech' and say something hateful about Elon Musk. That should turn your story into a total bin fire, in a good way.

INSTAGRAM. You'll need a sumptuous picture to go with your story. Instagram users typically want to see a tropical blue sky, a glimpse of someone's boutique brunch and a haughty cat gazing out to sea. Maybe slip the story to a nepo baby, tagged 'Unbelievable – how could anyone harm a dolphin?' They won't read it, but make sure they remember to add a link in bio to the story.

FACEBOOK. Get two polarised political accounts to paste the story directly into their feed. Title one 'IT'S NOT R COUNTRY ANYMORE!' with a row of Union Jack emojis and a lion. Title the other 'REVEALED: THE TORIES' SECRET DEAL WITH NAZI CANNIBALS' – then watch it ignite.

PINTEREST. The easiest way to extend your reach here is to slip your story into a complicated search phrase, such as 'BARGAIN POLITICAL MAKEOVER PET SCANDAL PROMPTS YUMMY CHICKEN CALL FOR ETHICAL JEWELLERY RESIGNATION'.

TIKTOK. Get some drill rapper with tattoos to spit the top three paragraphs of your story over a bone-shattering bassline, with a shimmering link to the full story that looks like a Keith Haring drawing.

ALL OTHER PLATFORMS. Just start a conspiracy thread about Russians releasing Donald Trump dick pics and include a link to your leaked story. But don't forget that you started the rumour, and embarrass yourself the next day by guilelessly sharing the story because you too have heard this rumour before, so there must be something to it.

The Paper Trail

People talk about 'British public opinion' as singular but, as with the media, British opinions are kaleidoscopically fractured. These opinions are also routinely said to be shaped by a 'right-wing press'. This is partially true, as the more hysterical newspapers are owned by some genuinely terrible bastards.

But physical newspapers are becoming a thing of the past. They've been steadily fading into dust and shadow as the internet media outlets have emerged from the chilly fog as enormous and obliterating as a Newfoundland iceberg. Editorials no longer land with that satisfying thud of freshly bundled newsprint. They appear noiselessly, electronically and simultaneously on devices that 150 years ago would have seemed terrifying, been recognised as the work of the Devil and treated as pure evil. Which only goes to prove, once again, that our ancestors were not as dim as we sometimes think.

Even though most newspapers have slithered across to the internet, the titles themselves – and the readership they carry – still matter. And the actual process of sucking up to the media has changed little from the twentieth century to the twenty-first. Here are some techniques.

The happy coincidence

It's important at all times to persuade yourself that what you're doing is not entering into anything as grubby as a 'deal' with media oligarchs. You are there merely to establish a human connection, to explore common areas of interest and to be sociable. This absolutely neutral meeting of minds often takes place:

★ over lunch or dinner (good luck trying to split the bill)
★ at a sporting event, where your companion will have VIP seats
★ in their amusing, discreet little nightclub at the top of the Shard
★ on their enormous yacht, which always has a woman's name
★ at their beautiful villa on the Amalfi Coast
★ at their landscaped nuclear bunker in New Zealand

It is true that your host would not actively oppose any changes in the law that would make their life more agreeable, but remember this is an equal, reciprocal relationship – you would not be averse to getting the support of a media empire, if that should for any reason occur. Life is serendipity, and you never know when the aims of your potential government and the interests of a media baron's readers, owners, investors, shareholders, subsidiary entities and financial managers might coincide.

The eyes have it

Online, things are more fluid. And you'll no doubt want to be the sort of prime minister who welcomes the egalitarian effects of the internet, and who rejects the notion that news coverage is in any sense 'dumbing down' as a result.

Oh, you'll probably say airily, there's an inordinate amount of talk about 'clicks and eyeballs' rather than 'readers', but have things really changed that much? When someone points to a photo of, say, a Tube carriage full of people staring at their screens, you might haughtily point out that the same scene a century ago would have shown passengers holding their newspapers at exactly the same angle.

The hierarchical structure of online news sources – and, let's face it, content aggregators who simply hoover up news from conventional sources and then repackage it for a younger and more impatient demographic – is skewed away from a traditional 'editor' and more towards 'chief financial officer' and 'head of memes'. Disdain the apparently trivial and ephemeral nature of online media at your peril. An Ofcom analysis of the news habits of sixteen- to twenty-four-year-olds reveals that traditional news sources like newspapers and radio might as well be ye olde town criers and the telegram.

Make yourself youthful

A whopping, perennially misunderstood, endlessly scrolling, constantly alert-for-gossip 83 per cent of young people get their news from online sources such as social media, podcasts, websites and online apps. Plus texts from their mates that start 'OMG WTF????' By far the biggest eyeball capture is on social media – 71 per cent, in fact. This is both disturbing and useful in equal measure if you're a would-be Leader of the Nation, for two reasons.

First, a lot of social media news dissemination is hasty and ill-considered. Young people may 'get their news' from social media, but a lot of the time they get it accidentally, browsing for something funny or shocking. Yes, this is disappointing in a way, but if that means targeting TikTok and Facebook with hollow bullshit that is funny or shocking and chimes with young people, that's what you're going to do. Can your media team make you funny? Maybe you have a head start by access to adorable pets doing silly things.

Or perhaps you have a knack for pranking people. Be careful. Social media users love pranking, but remember you're a politician. It doesn't fit your profile very well if you're going viral for duping, humiliating or actively harming people for a laugh. All that can wait until you're actually prime minister.

Second, the understanding is that social media platforms are neutral, accessible, egalitarian forums for the exchange of ideas... ha ha ha, please, like anyone believes that. Most of the clicks that take young people to a news source are on Google and Facebook, who will, in their curation and aggregation, try to align their content with whatever the hot topics are on social media. If you're really trying to reach young people, this is definitely the way in. You could start releasing – correction, 'dropping' – little hints online about the direction your premiership might take, all of which chime with young people's interests. Tell them you're looking seriously at reducing the voting age to sixteen, or incorporating beauty tutorials and Best Whale Explosions Ever into the school curriculum.

Old age pushovers

Older people, of course, will struggle to understand any social media campaign you and your team devise, which makes them perfect targets for all the scaremongering nonsense you're planning, so bear this in mind when formulating policy. Seriously, if old people are on social media they're halfway bamboozled already, so why not tell them that your political opponents will, if they get in at the next election:

★ abandon the pension triple-lock
★ commandeer OAPs' spare bedrooms for lodgers, to ease the housing shortage
★ slap a so-called 'can zero' tax on tinned food

- ★ end human checkouts in supermarkets by next year
- ★ replace winter fuel allowance with vouchers for Wagamama
- ★ compel all householders to take their own wheelie bins to a municipal tip
- ★ encourage pensioners to perform their own cataract operations
- ★ phase out pets, especially budgerigars
- ★ outlaw knick-knacks

An AI for an AI

Of course, as a potential prime minister acutely tuned into the ongoing media revolution, you'll know that it never stops. And yet another marvellous technological innovation is brutally rearranging the furniture on the deck of the News Titanic at the moment: artificial intelligence.

AI in this context is distinct from the artificial intelligence politicians deploy to pretend they're cleverer than they actually are. Media companies are now deploying AI-driven 'infotainment bottom-trawling' tools to aggregate content via dynamic paywalls, automated transcription, data analysis and chewy, flavourless prose.

This is good. In many ways, AI makes the potential synergy more resonant between an aspiring prime minister and an avaricious head of clickbait data farming (or editor). Far from disdaining your blatant scraping-together of policies and values and culture war inflection points to mould into a credible political platform, they're likely to give you a matey squeeze on the shoulder and recognise you as one of their own. The same sense of occult comradeship used to present itself as freemasonry, but times change. These days, if politicians and editors want the shared thrill of ritualised obeisance they become nutty monarchists, or join a church, or eat at Nando's.

TV Times

Although quite a lot of scheduled television has been superseded by streamers, and the very concept of 'live TV' has been reduced to breakfast news and harmless daytime shows, there is still an area of TV broadcasting where, sooner or later, as a potential PM you'll find yourself: the scapegoat slot.

Oh, you can schmooze your mates at the BBC, ITV, Channel 4 and the rest. They're in no position to help your career until you're actually prime minister. Then, perhaps, you might be tossed an easy interview with some non-threatening clot who's conscious that this is being flagged as an exclusive, so will keep it light.

But before that, at some point you will be the minister sent out to do the media round and forced to parrot the party line knowing that it's an outrageous lie or at the very least just a boring one. The only purpose of these interviews is for the questioner to express cartoonish incredulity at what you're saying and ask the same direct question over and over again. Obviously evasive techniques (see page 163) will help you, but think of it as the sort of mockery and degradation everybody had to go through at public school. I mean, the odds are that both you and the interviewer were privately educated and have a galloping sense of entitlement that usefully stands in for talent, so suck it up. (N.B. if you were state educated, now's your chance. Go rogue and start threatening physical violence. Counterthought: it's what the establishment expects, so don't.)

Once your political status is high and settled, you can start to gently put out feelers about fronting a TV show of your own when political fate has run its course (see page 218). But make sure you're available as a senior, knowledgeable politician for discussion programmes. Big-name TV journalists with shows named after them are always looking for potential PMs who will pretend to speak their mind on issues of the day. It will build your profile and, improbably, might make you seem more trustworthy.

Radio waves

Confusingly, quite a lot of radio is available to watch now. This is in the hope that a particularly embarrassingly and comical turn – you, possibly – will be available later as a clip that goes mad on the socials and reminds everyone that radio exists, sometimes in audio only!

Commercial radio phone-in clips are enormously popular online. Usually these feature the permanently scowling host, one headphone on and the other off, like some reluctant DJ who can't be bothered, and so has sat down. Usually they're looking astonished at the stupidity of whoever's calling in with thoughts about how low-emission zones are altering motorists' sperm count, or whatever.

A good schmooze here would be to befriend the station controller and persuade her or him to give you your own phone-in. Politicians have guested on phone-ins before with variable success, but you know, believe in yourself: yours could be the one that breaks the mould. You could perhaps be 'humorous', diffusing the anger and unhappiness of your callers with old-fashioned interjections – car horn, Swanee whistle, canned laughter – and deflect some of the personal attacks on your integrity by having a wacky sidekick who just repeats what the caller has said in a funny voice.

Castaway

Podcasts. Don't. Not until you've stopped being prime minister and you're rebuilding your image by turning yourself into someone affable and likeable. Podcasts, which are basically two people interrupting one another and laughing at their own jokes for forty-five minutes, will do you no good at all until the point where you have nothing left to lose, including your dignity and reputation.

The paper round

Newspapers are much easier to schmooze because they have specific human targets in post, a hangover from the twentieth century, when news was properly produced. Sub-editors would check grammar and sense. Editors would be endlessly available for lunch. Now that there are skeleton staffs and AI it's a lot more difficult, but newspapers still really matter. Even though everything ends up cut and pasted in social media, it's good to have some alliances with actual people.

Promised to exit the EU with or without a deal. He prorogued parliament – illegally, as later ruled by the Supreme Court – which limited the time available to debate Brexit. The Conservatives lost their working majority. A general election was called for December 2019 and the Conservatives won a majority of 80 seats, their biggest win since 1987 under Thatcher. Then the COVID-19 pandemic arrived, with Johnson attracting criticism for not attending emergency sessions of committees, for delaying lockdown and for mixed signalling about transmission of the virus.

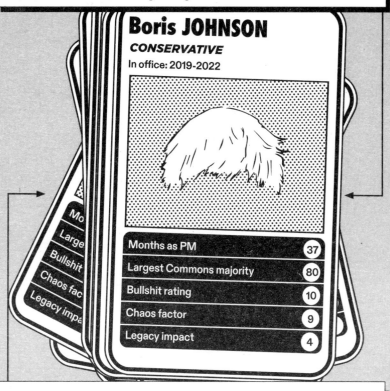

Boris JOHNSON
CONSERVATIVE
In office: 2019-2022

Months as PM	37
Largest Commons majority	80
Bullshit rating	10
Chaos factor	9
Legacy impact	4

In April 2022, Johnson was issued with a fixed penalty notice for breaching the COVID-19 lockdown regulations, becoming the first prime minister in British history to have been sanctioned for breaking the law while in office. An image of the Queen isolated at the funeral of the Duke of Edinburgh contrasted with revelations of parties at Number 10. He was accused of misleading Parliament, was hit by the resignation of thirteen ministers in twenty-four hours, and was finally forced to resign in July 2022. Vibe: partially collapsed tent.

Impressing the press

As any embittered former PM will tell you, it's always worth sucking up to newspapers, even the worst ones. Proprietors and editors need to know you're on their wavelength, even if you're not. It's okay to lie about your principles; a willingness to embrace untruths is one of the things you will definitely have in common. Maybe you could make this into a joke on your first encounter, which should be enhanced with your assumed personality, or an interesting companion, or an ingratiating gift, or all three. Good luck, and hold the front page – you're on your way!

Sidebar: it's worth mentioning local newspapers in passing, if only to remind ourselves that these days they are a sad, hollowed-out version of the once-mighty network of news that bound communities together in the olden days, before the internet nicked the advertising and atomised the entire world into individual phone-users. There are rarely any actual full-time staff on local newspapers, so really to make an impact you need to buy election wrap-arounds presented as newspaper pages, hymning your brilliance. Or, if it makes more economic sense, just buy the local newspaper.

Let the paper chase begin!

METRO. It's a free paper, and runs a lot of showbiz and entertainment news, so if you're having lunch with them, joke that free ones do exist (you're paying) and bring along a plus-one from *Love Island* or *Made in Chelsea*.

THE DAILY MAIL. Tell them you're related to the Duke of Buccleuch (they'll never check; everyone is). Don't demean yourself by slyly mentioning a political opponent's bingo wings or cellulite – they have very efficient infotainment AI tools for that.

THE TIMES. If you're looking to bond with anyone senior here, your safest bet is to suggest vegan barbecue or urban beagling.

THE TELEGRAPH. Arrive carrying a Marks & Spencer tote bag with (possibly) a human head in it, and talk about the War on Britain's History.

THE i and **THE INDEPENDENT.** Concert tickets to see a classic rock band at a National Trust property, or a vintage Kalashnikov, would make an ideal gift.

THE SUN. They're not interested in your gifts or your company at lunch, who the hell do you think you are? Pitch a column. Make it punchy, and specifically in contradiction of something you actually believe in (if you actually do).

THE DAILY MIRROR. Invite the features editor to a non-league football match and bring along a snooker celebrity as your plus-one. Go on to a rowdy pub and help break up a fight.

THE FINANCIAL TIMES. If you're inviting the editor to lunch, make sure the food element is replaced by axe-throwing or kick-boxing.

THE GUARDIAN. Take a principled stand on matters of fairness and justice but assure everyone involved that you stand absolutely no chance of becoming prime minister – you'll seem more interesting to them.

THE DAILY EXPRESS. Buy lunch for a senior manager, make sure they see your stab vest and be ready to explode in fury at something or other that doesn't matter. They love that.

THE MORNING STAR. Take along a big packed lunch and invite the editor to a local park to share it. Talk about the redistribution of wealth, and ask to borrow a fiver.

THE DAILY STAR. They're fun, they're trivial, they couldn't give a toss about politics. That makes them your primary target. Your best bet is lunchtime drinking somewhere with Sky Sports on a big screen.

Shortest serving PM ever, famously beaten in the end by her chief political rival, a lettuce. After a bafflingly rapid ascent through ministerial appointments – including a stretch as foreign secretary notable for a series of weird, moody and aggrandising official photographs – Truss took over as PM on 6 September 6th 2022, after beating Rishi Sunak in a party membership vote.

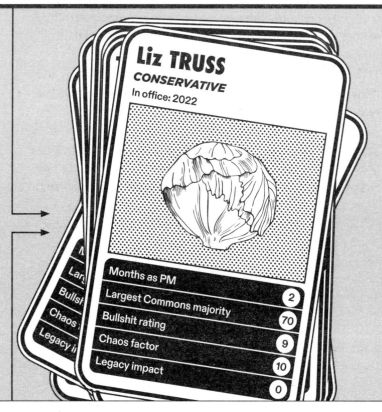

Liz TRUSS

CONSERVATIVE
In office: 2022

Months as PM	2
Largest Commons majority	70
Bullshit rating	9
Chaos factor	10
Legacy impact	0

She announced a cap on household energy bills, costed at up to £140 billion over two years. Then her Chancellor Kwasi Kwarteng unveiled a mini-budget which proposed slashing taxes, borrowing heavily, and stimulating growth. The economy crashed, the pound tanked, falling to its lowest ever rate against the US dollar – $1.033. Truss first defended the budget, then reversed some of it, defended Kwarteng, then sacked him. She became the most unpopular prime minister in British history, and was forced to resign after less than two months. Vibe: comedy ghost.

Create the headlines you want to see

Everyone in the media is familiar with manifesting, where you simply write down on a piece of paper what you want – a million pounds, good health, peace in the Middle East – then put it in the drawer. And then it happens, although usually only when you're rich, healthy and live in Saudi Arabia.

However, it does no harm to visualise the sort of headlines you'd like to see about yourself. It gives you a goal to work back from – imagining the sort of policies you'd like to champion and the sort of prime minister you'd like to be remembered as. Also, since we've firmly established that you're a narcissist, it gives your ego a well-deserved coddling.

Imagine the person in these headlines on the opposite page is the future you. Cor, yeah! Which headline captures the essential you?

RELIEF AS CHILD RESCUED BY THE PM FROM SAVAGE DOG ATTACK MAKES FULL RECOVERY

EU MEMBER STATES PLEAD WITH PM TO LEAD BRITAIN BACK INTO EUROPE

Sir Paul praises PM's guitar solo on latest reconstructed Beatles song as 'beyond fab'

'This is for Britain' vows PM as he auctions Nobel Peace prize for charity

PM wins fight in Commons car park with notorious American neo-Nazi

PM insists doubling of GDP in six months is 'thanks to hard-working Britons'

BLIND MAN 'SEES CLEARLY AGAIN' AFTER TOUCHING PHOTO OF PM IN SWIMMING COSTUME

The Pope calls PM 'the saviour humanity needs' in heartfelt Christmas address

Headline generator

When you see how easy it is to put together a tabloid headline, you begin to understand how important it is to stay on the right side of the media.

Have a go by choosing the components that correspond with the first letter of your first name in the first column, the first letter of your favourite politician's name in the middle column and the first letter of your constituency in the last column.

	FIRST LETTER OF YOUR FIRST NAME	FIRST LETTER OF YOUR FAVOURITE POLITICIAN'S NAME	FIRST LETTER OF YOUR CONSTITUENCY
A	PM denies knowledge of	nude breakfast with	the 'blokerati'
B	PM supports	undermining	obese constituents
C	PM confirms	rising cost of	dogging OAPs
D	PM plays down	death threats from	own family
E	PM talks up	harsher penalties for	flatulent cows
F	PM considers	plans to step back from	sex workers
G	PM to prioritise	alliance with	hallucinated demons
H	PM 'relaxed' about	malign influence of	'thought plagiarism'
I	PM to talk about	'regrettable' actions of	gambling cartel

J	PM laughs off	relationship with	TV hypnotists
K	PM avoids questions about	mum's caravan full of	engorged civil servants
L	PM slams	poor fashion choices of	*Celebrity Mastermind* contestants
M	PM defends claims over	an internet teeming with lies about	'cancer do-gooders'
N	PM complains about	invisible brainwaves from	AI sexbots
O	PM's anger over	book revelations about	emotional support animals
P	PM dismisses rumours of	oiled paddling pool 'larks' with	public school head in Nazi uniform
Q	PM seeking legal advice over	sharing platform with	Liberal Democrats
R	PM buoyant despite	links to	Prince of Wales
S	PM's shock confession:	posting of leaked naked video of	'shaved cats'
T	PM's sister refuses to comment on	cocaine-crazed	'corpses of enemies'
U	PM to tell King about	shaming evidence of	NSFW manga furries
V	PM to call press conference about	obscene drawings of	penis 'puppetry'
W	PM's 'no comment' on	'drunken antics' of	butlers at Buckingham Palace
X	PM's gardener reveals	gay university pal's obsession with	weird games in Cabinet Room
Y	PM's announces inquiry into	compromising photographs of	Prince and Princess of Wales
Z	PM 'not aware of'	hush-money to bury story about	erotic dancing wonks

A Very British COO

We've all seen a beleaguered PM – savagely attacked by His Majesty's loyal opposition, derided in the media, undermined by their own party's restlessness for a change at the top – and thought: 'Why are you limping on like this? Why not chuck it in and find happiness somewhere else?' And then we realise: they're addicted to it. They *need* to be PM.

Are need and an addictive personality ideal prime ministerial characteristics? They are not. But the job does seem to encourage desperate behaviour. And unfortunately, it's only a matter of time before some devious chancer of a PM finds a way of gaming Britain's notoriously vague constitution. That devious chancer could be you. Because at some point you'll be asking yourself: Hmm – just how ruthless would I like to be?

One's Audience of One

Imagine you've been prime minister for a while. The excitement has gone. You're trudging along for the weekly audience with the king, month after month. By now, a prime minister would surely be able to sense whether they and the monarch shared common values. And if you clicked, the weekly audience might feel more like both of you checking in with your therapist. You tell the king how your week's been – party loyalty gone to shit, poll numbers through the floor – and he tells you about his: infantilised by the press, ignored by the legislature, and so on.

And then it occurs to you both at the same time. Whose side would the military be on, if it came to it? The monarch – who, let's remember, has served in the navy and is Commander in Chief of the Armed Forces – and his best friend the prime minister? Or Parliament, a Gothic barn full of self-serving, time-serving windbags?

Yes: unthinkable. As are so many things, until they are thought. What, after all, is the 'royal prerogative'? It is only loosely defined by custom and convention, so it's ideal for your crafty plan. The king has 'authority, privilege and immunity' as sovereign – on paper, at least. Since the nineteenth century, by convention, the advice of the prime minister or the Cabinet – who are then accountable to Parliament for the decision – has been required in order for the royal prerogative to be exercised. The monarch remains constitutionally empowered to exercise the royal prerogative against the advice of the prime minister or the Cabinet, but in practice would only do so in emergencies, or where existing precedent does not adequately apply to the circumstances in question.

Exactly: thinkable. You made it to Downing Street – of course you did, everyone always believed in you – and you've become best mates with the king. What mischief might you cook up, you and the Commander in Chief of the Armed Forces? It would have to be a perfectly fair rethinking of current arrangements, a power-sharing deal with the king as a sort of Chief Executive of the UK, and you as Chief Operating Officer. The prime minister as a Very British COO.

Of course, you're thinking, 'I couldn't possibly take part in some sort of fascist coup, who do you take me for?' and you'd be right. It's up to you and the king to decide what constitutes an emergency. Perhaps the country, in your view, is becoming *too* fascist or racist, or just too dull and miserable. Perhaps the economy simply isn't trickling down money fast enough to the people who need it most. Perhaps the embedded inequalities in the system urgently require a new social template, and the only way to achieve that is by seizing the assets and freezing the bank accounts of (again, just illustratively,) tax-dodgers, unscrupulous landlords, PPE profiteers, shareholders of public utilities and, let's face it, the extended royal family.

Would the king be up for it? Given all he's been through, you bet. But he needs to trust you, to know that you both share the same Vision of Britain, as he once called it when he was merely a tetchy Prince of Wales. So if you're serious about converting your prime ministership into a bloodless coup, you need to suck up to the sovereign asap. These are some of his passions: make sure you share them.

Architecture. There was a huge fuss back in the 1980s when Charles started moaning – directly to architects sometimes – about the parlous state of new architecture. 'Why has everything got to be vertical, straight, unbending, only at right angles – and functional?' he famously asked, shortly before every city skyline morphed into an anthology of weird, curvy, bulbous lumps. Whatever: just make sure to be firmly nostalgic for any architecture that existed before Beethoven. Let him rant on and on about the commodity, firmness and delight of architecture and nod gravely, as if you give a flying toss.

Religion. Charles has always wanted to be Defender of 'Faith', not 'the Faith', and has talked up diversity and multiculturalism. But he inherits an increasingly secular kingdom. At the turn of the century, more than 70 per cent of adults identified as Christian; only around 45 per cent do now. And although there has been an increase in members of other faiths, Britain's official religion now is atheism. You and the king might usefully discuss ways of making the Church of England's land holdings and buildings more useful. Churches, for example, might once again be places of sanctuary, where vicars would be empowered to tell the Home Office to fuck off.

A modernised royal family. Yes, he may have traditional and conservative tastes, but the king has repeatedly said he wants to modernise 'the Firm'. As COO/PM you might gently suggest to the CEO/king that in order to modernise, the monarchy should be nationalised. Here too your exciting, tyrannical-yet-benevolent joint government will find a rich seam to mine. The monarchy holds declared assets worth north of £22 billion, and God knows what else they've got squirrelled away. Charles says he wants less pomp and circumstance, so you could probably stick all the unworn ceremonial clothes on Vinted and make a fortune. Also, wouldn't Buckingham Palace make a brilliant behemoth of a boutique hotel?

Other topics to explore your shared interest in: homeopathy, fountain pens, adultery, tree-planting, watercolours, the Goons, organic vegetables.

Your First Year as PM

The advice from every former prime minister looking back at their time in office is identical. Push through as much as you can in the first year. It's imperative to make your mark as quickly as possible. After Year One it becomes more difficult to build legislative momentum. A great deal of your time will be spent trying to reverse the avalanche of hostile press coverage and heal the very public divisions in your own party. You can't afford to squander any time.

Here are the core objectives for your first year as leader of the greatest little island country this side of Iceland:

★ **Nickname.** Lock your entire team of advisers away until they've come up with a great nickname. It needs to sound like something a mischievous journalist has come up with. So it can't be too flattering: 'Miracle Woman', 'The Healer', 'Our Beloved Leader'. Nor too sarcastic: 'Der Führer', 'Miseryguts', 'Wanker'. You want neutral yet affectionate: 'Steady', 'Safe Pair', 'Nice One', 'Coach', 'Top Cat', or just your name truncated with a chummy '-y' at the end, e.g. 'Starmy'.

★ **Start a war.** And finish it, by winning it. Once again we're reading from the Margaret Hilda Thatcher Playbook. Despite Conservative jubilation in the wake of the 1979 election win, her popularity started to tank quite early on. Then Argentina invaded the Falkland Islands, Britain snatched them back and the Bride of Frankenstein's stock soared. So could yours. Ideally your war should be mostly rhetoric and posturing; nobody wants an actual shooting war. Choose your enemy wisely. You need someone who likes to chat shit about Britain (or England anyway) but doesn't have much in the way of military capability. So like Ireland, or the Federated States of Micronesia. By all means start a ruck with the Vatican City but NB try to leave religion out of it.

★ **Make yourself imitable.** You need to be a memorable prime minister, which means meeting impressionists halfway with top-quality catchphrases and mannerisms that a) don't make you look like a complete fucking berk but b) may be affectionately mimicked by young, shouty, tightly edited YouTubers. Look at any mannerisms you have and then gently amplify them to 'adorable' level. Catchphrases should be snappy and of the moment, e.g:

SHIELDS UP, LET'S GO!   POVERTY? FUCK OFF!

HANDS!

WHAT WE DO, WHO WE ARE!   OK! LET'S WALK THE DOG AND BAG UP THE SHIT

POLITIKS, POLITOKS!

★ **Celebrity endorsements.** Any sensible high-profile PM welcomes the extra pizzazz a showbiz supporter brings. But your team will need to vet them before you reciprocate. And by vet, let's be clear. The last thing you want as prime minister is to have a picture of you and the celeb laughing it up, only for a story to break about their disgraceful, sexually debauched past, polluting your reputation with their toxic fallout. The vetting process is therefore fairly straightforward: female celebrities only.

As Chancellor he launched the Eat Out To Help Out scheme to boost the hospitality sector during the Covid pandemic, which it also boosted. After Truss's resignation he put himself forward in a frictionless leadership race after Boris Johnson ruled himself out and Penny Mordaunt withdrew. He took over in October 2022. Known for his technocratic, pragmatic approach, he steadily lost popular support but doubled down on his flagship immigration scheme to have migrants and asylum seekers sent to Rwanda for 'processing'.

Rishi SUNAK
CONSERVATIVE
In office: 2022-2024

SKY

Months as PM	21
Largest Commons majority	73
Bullshit rating	7
Chaos factor	3
Legacy impact	1

As the cost of living became a political hot topic, his wealth, several homes and revelations about the business dealings of Infosys, his father-in-law's company, further damaged his reputation. Vibe: absconding crypto trader.

CHAPTER 10:
YOUR PM
AFTERLIFE

Anyone who's serious about becoming prime minister needs to think ahead, especially to the time when they're no longer prime minister.

Nothing lasts for ever. Unless your period as Glorious Leader ends in tearful thanks from a grateful nation (not totally impossible: you have roughly a 1 in 2.8 billion chance of that happening) you'll need to plan an exit route. Ideally, this should be the first item on your agenda on your very first day in office, as it's never too early to start thinking beyond life at the top.

You Are Your Skillset

Some of the easiest afterlife money to be made is in those weird little 'strategic consultancy' roles that require you to turn up for thirty hours a year and are worth three times your annual prime ministerial salary. The non-executive directorships, the advisory roles, the loosely-defined vice-presidencies for special projects. The reason these corporations will pay you a fortune is not your expertise but your trophy prestige as a former PM. Of course, this always works better abroad, where people will be less familiar with your actual performance as prime minister.

You and your new employers will share the charming conceit that because you headed a Cabinet for five years you have a magical understanding of the fabled 'interworld' where politics and the commercial world exist in a kind of freeport Narnia. When in fact everybody understands what your status is: a politician with excellent contacts and an exploitable backstory. It's already commonplace now for ministers to leave their specific regulatory 'area of expertise' and glide into the corresponding commercial field. A secretary of state for health might usefully find their ultimate commercial destiny working for a private health provider aggressively seeking succulent, low-risk bits of the NHS to bite off. A minister for social care would be an asset for the residential home operator looking to crowd local authorities out of the market. As an ex-PM, you'd just be doing the same – more importantly, of course – in an already contextualised reality.

The Next Stage

What is a former PM's 'area of expertise', exactly? Well, it's quite a broad brief, so there's no harm in that area being 'everything', is there? It makes perfect theoretical sense to be working for people bidding for government contracts in everything from giant infrastructure projects to catering, as you must surely have some perspective as a former PM on roads and dinners. It's simply new you pitching to old you. And all that carping about poachers and gamekeepers from jealous moralisers? Please. You're an ex-PM. You didn't create this world, you're simply living in it.

Perhaps it's the showing-off you'll miss. Understandable: your sudden disappearance from the media top story slots will be brutal, even if in your last days at Number 10 the headlines were all 'Pressure builds for PM to resign' and 'Chaos and recriminations as bitter PM accepts defeat'. Luckily, there's a whole world waiting for thwarted narcissists who still want to be noticed.

The Right Thing

As recent former PMs have found, the international lecture circuit is a lucrative one. Prime ministers, once they're in office and casting around for a well-paid afterlife, discover a global network of current and former heads of state. Some will still be lecturing. Some will be getting older and, as with retired sportspeople, will be moving into coaching and possibly even becoming an agent, smoothing the way for others at a rate of 10 per cent. The international lecture circuits are well-travelled routes, not dissimilar to those taken by space satellites, going round and round the world, sending out a steady, unwavering signal. Think of your PM afterlife as an outer space waiting to be explored, with you as another glittering lump of political debris in permanent orbit.

It should go without saying that the more outrageous you're prepared to be, the greater the rewards. And it's no secret that there's a great deal more money to be made on the right than on the left. Radical leftists might include fairly harmless former centre-left politicians who miss the limelight; once safely out of active politics, they're free to go full-on Marxist Terminator. But unless they have rock-star looks or a bestselling book to punt, the circuit they'll be on is one of draughty halls and forlorn civic buildings, with a closet for a dressing room and expenses plus a whip-round.

Whereas all over the world, and especially in America, the further you go right-wingnut the more lucrative it is. Audiences are hungry for stories of conspiracy and betrayal to help make sense of their lives. Delusional accounts of culture wars and how you won them, even if you actually lost them, are at a premium. Honestly, one of the very few upsides of living in a post-truth world is that you can say anything you like in the US: just make it up, the madder the better. And if a US president likes you, opens a few doors for you, then maybe you can reciprocate by smoothing visas for his armed guard when he does a reading at Cheltenham Book Festival.

Hot-ticket paranoia-based speech subjects currently ringing up the $$$:

★ Every civil service in the world has been infiltrated by left-wing extremists whose main mission, possibly co-ordinated by a left-wing extremist HQ Somewhere In Europe, is to destroy that civil service from the inside. Yes, dismantling everything, including the extremist civil servants' salaries, pensions and job prospects.

★ There is a secret network of liberal politicians, paediatricians and vegans who are kidnapping interns, children and iron-rich pulses to form a 'sleeper army' sworn to kill conservative parents who 'identify as carnivores'.

★ There is a Final War coming between the People of the Sun and the People of the Moon. The public doesn't know who the good guys are. The bad guys don't know either. But the good guys – the speaker and their audience – already know they are the good guys, so Moon, Sun – who cares?

★ All vaccinations contain a 'mind virus' – possibly originating in a Chinese laboratory – that makes you want another one in a year's time. Each new jab updates the software, which transmits a wetware data readout to Hillary Clinton and her mates. Why? You tell me. YOU TELL ME.

★ Birds don't exist. They're figments of our imaginations. And our imaginations are in turn being controlled by mysterious Dream Engines disguised as smart speakers in preparation for the day when Taylor Swift (swifts don't exist!) is revealed to be the world's first cyborg to pass as human, and the signal is given to kill anyone with a tattoo, however discreet.

Some people lap this stuff up, because some people believe that gullibility is a superpower. But perhaps instead of talking bollocks to the wilfully stupid, you'd like to carry on making the world a better place now you're out of office. In fact, why not put that as your 'out of office' message on emails? 'Sorry I can't respond to your email as I am currently out of office, making the world a better place.'

That certainly seems to be the trajectory of former prime minister Tony Blair. The Tony Blair Institute for Global Change made £65m in 2021, which certainly isn't global small change, is it? The former PM has said he wants the institute 'to be entrepreneurial, agile and give governments good solid advice'.

In fact, former Finnish prime minister Sanna Marin has joined the institute as an adviser, a comforting indication of a possible future for former PMs around the world, who one day might all be joining one another's institutes. Maybe you should start thinking about forming your own institute. After all, if you can work with any government, the world's your champagne and oyster bar. Just call your institute something worthy and charge thirty grand a day.

Non-Executive Summary

In the end, you'll be fine. Remember, you owe nothing to anyone, and certainly not to your party or the electorate. If you're a former prime minister, either you'd had enough of them, or vice versa. It's only fair that you now cash in on all that hard work: the endless meetings, the eternity of briefing breakfasts, micro-lunches, VIP dinners and drinks parties with the most boring yet confident people in the world. Goodbye public service, hello self-curated afterlife.

As leader of His Majesty's Opposition, has now looked with disdain on three prime ministers in fairly rapid succession. A former Director of Public Prosecutions, he has a long legal background and a long legal face to go with it. His dull demeanour has so far been his most effective political attribute: an undertaker's seriousness after the cartoon antics of Johnson, Truss and Sunak. He won a stonking 174-seat majority in the general election of 2024 and was even seen to smile briefly on his way in to Number 10.

Keir STARMER

LABOUR

In office: 2024–

Months as PM	?
Largest Commons majority	?
Bullshit rating	?
Chaos factor	?
Legacy impact	?

He has pledged a programme of national renewal. His government's first act was to scrap the controversial Rwanda scheme, and he approved the swift and decisive sentencing of race rioters in August 2024. So far he has very much played to his strengths: a droning whine of a voice, a tense and awkward persona at press conferences, an emphasis on hard work and an allergy to any sense of fun. Vibe: mildly outraged pharmacist.

WHAT WILL YOU DO AFTER BEING PM?

Do you want to be remembered as a philanthropist?

Oh yeah → *OK, no not really*

Right but are you one?

Absolutely

AND make money?

Yes *No*

Go back to 'fuck that, show me the money'

YOU'RE A SAINT, OR IN SOME SORT OF RECOVERY

FIND (OR START) AN INSTITUTION WITH 'GLOBAL' IN THE TITLE

TV PERSONALITY

Fuck that, show me the money → *Just biz?*

Show business or Showbiz?

Do you have a work ethic?

Public speaking

Media

Go madder

Yes

No

TV POLITICAL HEAVY WEIGHT

Become voice of reason

USE LEVERAGE TO FUND START-UPS

TED TALKS, INSPIRATIONAL PODCASTS

US CIRCUIT

MONETISE SELF, TAKE A LOAD OF 3-DAYS-PER-ANNUM GIGS

QUIZ: HOW PM ARE YOU?

Now that you've seen what it takes to be prime minister, are you sure you have the right instincts and the correct psychological impulses? A split-second decision can mean the difference between dazzling, golden triumph or abject, shit-coloured fucktastrophe.

Here comes the final test, to discover whether you've got it or not. Multiple-choice decisions will give you an entirely dependable assessment of whether you're cut out for this. You'll need your wits about you. If your results are not in the top 10 per cent of respondents then, alas, your journey may be over. If, however, you do make it through, you're clearly one to watch. Good luck!

A journalist from the Daily Mirror *calls you. An intern you employed years ago is now claiming that you sexted her. It gets worse: she claims she received unsolicited pictures of your actual sex bits. What do you do?*

1. Furiously deny the allegation, say the sex bits must belong to someone else and send the journalist a picture of your own sex bits to prove it.

2. Neither admit nor deny the allegation, and say you cannot recall that particular dispatch of genital imagery.

3. Say you can't remember as it was so long ago (even if six months), and that those were very different times for vaginas and penises.

4. Take out a super-injunction to stop publication of the story, tell the journalist (strictly off the record) that the former intern is trying to capitalise on an honest mistake: the photo was intended for your urologist.

Decision B

There's a simmering row between Britain and France over border security. The President of France has described your position as 'myopic ethno-nationalism'. How do you respond?

1. With sadness, that he should seek to make political capital out of human misery. In your view, neighbouring countries should collaborate, not agitate.

2. With sadness, that this issue should be weaponised with French elections coming up, and with such a pretentious phrase.

3. Call the President of France a 'two-faced arsehole, and you can quote me on that'.

4. Say you're flying to Paris for urgent talks aimed at de-escalating the situation and preventing war with France, 'which unfortunately a sizeable minority of British people still want'.

Decision C

You're addressing an audience of industrialists when a pair of climate-change protesters storm the stage, shout slogans in posh voices and hurl glitter over you. What's your reaction?

1. As security are bundling them out, observe drily: 'There we are, ladies and gentlemen. Another excellent argument for state education.'

2. Embrace the moment and launch into an Abba song.

3. Do a hands-out shrug and say 'I guess activism is showbusiness for ugly people!'

4. Give the signal to your aide, who tosses you a super-soaker, which you expertly catch. Squirt it at the protesters and tell the audience defiantly: 'And that's why I always have this baby full of my own piss and ready to go!'

The Governor of the Bank of England rings at 3 a.m. The Gold Reserve cannot be located. It's been either mislaid or stolen. There has to be an announcement; the news is bound to leak. You scramble the Press Team: 'Right, what do we say? Apart from, there's nothing to worry about?'

1. My government and I, after consultations with the Chancellor and a team from the Treasury, have taken the bold decision to electronically transfer the entire value of the UK's gold reserves into a form of Bitcoin called Popcoin. Just in case anything happens in the future that I will certainly have no knowledge of.

2. These allegations are wholly untrue. The gold exists in a location so secret I couldn't even tell you if I wanted to, which I don't. I think the British people want to focus on something that really matters, such as immigration or the weather, and not on some silly game of Gold-Reserve Battleships!

3. There has been a temporary, and wholly repairable, glitch in the Gold Reserve IT system. Clearly the search result 'Total Gold Reserve Value: £0' is a nonsense, and our technical engineers are working round the clock to get everything back up and running as quickly as possible.

4. First, let me assure you: the gold has not been stolen. It remains the property of the United Kingdom, wherever it may be. Indeed, wherever it actually is. I just wish you media guys didn't relentlessly keep talking our beautiful country down. Instead of asking 'where's our fucking gold?' – which is not just negative, but also extremely rude – why is nobody saying 'look at all the lovely silver we have, safe as houses: look at it all!'

5. I have been very clear: the suggestion that we – that anyone – could lose, through negligence or theft or forgetfulness, billions and billions and billions of pounds' worth of gold, is as preposterous as it is defamatory, calling into question as it does the efficacy and diligence of the Bank of England, and it is a suggestion I and my government will start again from the top, just to be sure we're all on the same page here, so let me repeat that I have been very clear: the suggestion that we – that anyone – could lose, through negligence or theft or forgetfulness, billions and billions and billions of pounds' worth of gold is as preposterous as it is defamatory, calling into question as it does the efficacy and diligence of the Bank of England...

Decision E

You're being interviewed on a London talk-radio programme. The conversation suddenly veers off from the contentious issue of 20 mph speed limits into the even more contentious issue of ultra-low emission zones. You address this urbanely by saying that you recognise the argument from both sides, that personal vehicle preference and air quality are always tricky to balance, and that in the end it will be the will of the people. A live on-air caller accuses you of being poorly briefed on this subject. You assure them you are monitoring this issue closely. They then challenge you to tell listeners what the ULEZ vehicle pollution level is. You don't know. Do you:

1. Say 'Sorry, I'm not going to get drawn into just flinging numbers about. The threshold has been scientifically arrived at, let's weigh the social impact, the pros and cons.'

2. Say 'Well, you tell me, you obviously have the information there. And please tell me if you think it's too much or too little. I'm listening.'

3. Say 'It doesn't matter if it's 10 or if it's 10,000 or whatever it is, decimal places or not. We need consensus, and that doesn't have a number, it has a quality.'

4. Say 'Hold on...' and then, in full view of the phone-in host, hold your mobile in the air, read a text that's just come in and say 'It's 75g/km of C02 emissions per vehicle. I'm reading that off a text because I have a very efficient team who keep me briefed. Anyway, that's the number, what's your fucking point, smuggo?'

Decision F

You're doing a tour of a shopping centre that has seen better days. To show you're not a massive snob, you lead your team, and accompanying press mob, into a shop called Everything's a Pound, Everything — Nothing Costs More Than One Pound. Once you're in, of course, you have to buy something. Already one of your comms team has reminded you not to ask how much it is. But which item do you choose? Careful. You will be judged. What are you taking to the checkout?

1. An inflatable tenth-size Ford Focus.

2. A '100% accurate' pregnancy test.

3. A plastic Take That spaghetti fork.

4. A ceramic giraffe in an Aston Villa shirt.

5. A packet of 'genuine vajazzles'.

Decision G

You stupidly agreed to do a 'Meet the Kids' spot on CBBC. They can ask you anything, and the producers refused your request to see the questions in advance. A bright-looking lad of about twelve, in a little gilet, puts his hand up. You invite his question: 'We've been doing twentieth-century history and I wanted to know, if you could have dinner with just one dictator out of Hitler, Stalin, Mussolini, Mao or Pol Pot, who would you invite, and what would you do for their dinner?' Huge applause for this little shit's question. How do you answer him?

1. Say you'd have Hitler over, do him a nice nut roast, and just as you're about to carve, you'd stab him to death.

2. Say you'd have Mao over, order in a Chinese Feast for Two, stab him to death and eat all the food yourself.

3. Say you'd have Stalin over, serve drugged vodka, no dinner, lock him in the cellar and go on holiday for a few months while he starves to death.

4. Invite them all over, maybe a sort of picnic spread, cold meats, potato salad and that. Using a universal translator app, encourage everyone to discuss the notion of dictatorship, the ups and downs and so on, and stealthily but surely get everyone to agree that the industrial slaughter of millions of people is really very bad, and democratic principles and peace and working together is super good. Then get your podcast team to set up a meeting for a project with the working title *The Rest Is Genocide*.

Decision H

It was bound to happen, sooner or later. A terrible, terrible poem you wrote for a student magazine has been dug up and is now being viciously mocked by your simpering, sniggering enemies. It's written in the then-fashionable (now-irritating) unpunctuated style. Worse, it celebrates bizarre sexual goings-on and the powerful effects of exotic and illegal drugs. You call a snap press conference. What's your angle?

1. Laughingly dismiss the poem as youthful folly, say you've matured and now confine yourself to (properly punctuated) limericks, to wit:

> *When young, with a haircut quite sinister,*
> *and no prospect of being prime minister,*
> *I took lots of drugs, drank vodka from mugs,*
> *now my meds are all I self-administer.*

2. Recall the mescaline with fondness, explaining how it revealed the interconnectedness of everything in the universe, a bit like how the civil service works.

3. Say it shows that Britain can mould the most unpromising human material into someone who believes that everyone matters.

4. Accuse your critics of 'synthetic outrage' and say they're doing what all miserable gits do: talk down our brilliant young people, rather than cherishing them as our nation's future.

You're visiting a school with a media gaggle in tow, hoping to look vaguely human and normal. The media team brief was to concoct a light and breezy conversation with baffled, distracted seven-year-olds and try not to sound like a Martian trying to pass as human. Into the classroom you go. A lot of sceptical little faces. You sidle over to a table, crouch down awkwardly, introduce yourself. Obviously the kids do not give a fuck.

'Hello! What's your name? Chloe, that's... sorry, Zoe. That's a great drawing, very good. Oh, it's me? Ah, you've all drawn pictures of me! I love the hat, it's... oh, that's a piano, is it? Dropped on my head? Well, that's quite naughty, actually, who would drop...? Oh, all the teachers because they hate me? I'm dead, am I? Okay, Theo, did the camera guys pick that up, shit, can we go out and come in again? Oh, the mic, yeah. Bollocks...'

And now the media have you muttering 'shit' in a classroom. How the bollocks are you going to get out of this?

1. Leave. Just leave, really quickly. Urgent business. Mop up the 'shit' later.

2. Stay. Brazen it out. Pretend you said 'that's it'. Shoot the class teacher a baleful glare as you say out loud that you're more interested in teachers being accessories to brutal imaginary murder. This is a serious issue. I mean, how young do they have to be before we don't encourage them to represent the death by crushing of a senior politician? I shall be contacting the police about this hate crime.

3. Go back to Zoe. Find a piece of paper and a pen, start drawing. 'Zoe, I think it's a bit mean to drop a piano on someone. That could really hurt. What could we drop on them that would be funny and not hurt?' You think, deeply. 'A fish? An egg? Some (shhh) dog poo?' Zoe laughs.

4. Go back to Zoe. Say you think a piano is too heavy, what about some

cheese slices? 'Oh, and who should we drop them on? Let's think... a policeman? The lollipop lady? Your head teacher?'

You're going through a bad patch, polling lower than any prime minister in history. Nothing seems to be cutting through. 'What I really need', you rashly say to your comms team, 'is a dead-cat bounce.'

Oh DEAR. The next time you see comms, they're all looking very pleased with themselves — apart from the comms chief, who sits ashen-faced. Apparently one of your junior spads, Hugo, took it upon himself to murder Barry, the Downing Street cat. The body has been disposed of, allowing you — so he reasoned — to gain political bounce via the dead cat and the grief and compassion you'll share with the nation. After an awkward and protracted silence, followed by a brief explanation of the dead cat analogy, a peremptory sacking and a reminder about the non-disclosure agreement Hugo signed, you hold an emergency session. Clearly Barry's not coming back. You issue a statement that says:

1. Barry was kidnapped by mysterious political opponents and killed when you refused to pay the ransom: the government does not bargain with terrorists. Barry is now a martyr, and a symbol of Britain's 'independent catlike spirit'.

2. Barry died of natural causes. There will be a Service of Remembrance in Westminster Abbey, to which the world's leading politicians and their pets have been invited.

3. Barry died 'doing what he loved best': sleeping. It was a very gentle exit from this world, as nobody noticed for quite a while.

4. Barry has gone missing, so you have asked all householders in the Whitehall area to check their sheds, idle Daimlers, servants' quarters and sex dungeons. Flyers have been posted throughout St James's Park with a photograph of Barry looking imperious outside Number 10, and an artist's impression of what a feral Barry might look like now.

Obviously Number 10 now needs a new pet. Britons are famously a nation of animal lovers, what's past is past, and pictures of you with the new (unmurdered) Downing Street mascot are bound to boost your image. Too bad about Barry, but let's move on: you need a new photogenic pet you can be seen with. There's a potential three to four points of personal popularity rating in it, so choose wisely. You announce that the new prime ministerial animal will be:

1. A bigger, better cat. A panther, say. Even better, a lioness. She could be paraded around London in a Union Jack onesie on an open-top bus every time the Lionesses win a game of football.

2. A tortoise and a hare. They could be presented by the Chancellor of the Exchequer before every Budget as a reminder that economic recovery is a marathon, not a sprint.

3. A miniature pony called Brenda. She can graze in the Number 10 gardens most of the week, but every Wednesday you and Brenda will walk the short distance between Downing Street and the House of Commons for Prime Minister's Questions, where her presence as an emotional-support animal should discourage people from shouting at you.

4. A dog. Dogs are loyal, like your backbenchers. Nothing too EU, obviously, like a dachshund or a French poodle. A border collie, say. Anything that will be obedient and associate you in the minds of the public with having a masterful grip on public affairs, bagging up the bad stuff for Britain and disposing of it properly.

5. Something exotic. An alligator, say. Or a monitor lizard. Or a royal python. It might make you look charmingly eccentric and up for anything.

Another carefully choreographed photo opportunity at a factory in the Midlands that makes bin liners. You get a quick guided tour of the premises wearing regulation safety gear – this makes anyone wearing it look as though they might do a proper job for a living. To follow, a short press conference at which the PM will talk about consigning political opponents to the 'dustbin of history', then, brandishing a handful of bin liners, will say: 'And let me tell you, Britain has the means to do it properly!' Followed by invited questions on the economy. This is a clever trap, as there's an unpublished Treasury report which shows improvement in some areas and the prime minister is going to give everyone the good news in a relaxed, upbeat way. It will be a galloping triumph.

Unfortunately, as you grab a handful of bin liners, mentally rehearsing the terrible dad jokes that will lead into the Treasury report, there's breaking news. A junior minister in the department for education has been caught in a sting, offering access to the prime minister for a consulting fee of five grand an hour. The first question at the press conference is about the treachery of the junior minister. All anyone wants to ask about is the sting. Your prime ministerial smile is stretched tighter than a snare drum. You gurgle and stutter. You make weird drowning noises. It's a calamity. It's a catastrophe. It'll be all over social media, on a loop, set to music. People on TikTok will be doing little dances to it. What do you do?

1. Look around, counting the number of people in the room. Say 'Okay, you guys need to have a whip round: that's 350 grand you owe me, ha ha ha!'

2. Give a relaxed laugh, saying you know all about it: that it was a 'boomerang sting' and the junior minister had full knowledge of it. It was set up deliberately to trap journalists who think their job is to entrap ministers of the Crown when in fact their job is to report the truth. This story is a lie, and it's one we made up. Shame on you, the media. Shame on you.

3. Say 'God, people are going to be dancing to this on TikTok later, aren't they?' and then do a little dance. Make sure your dance is the one people will remember.

4. Say you can't possibly comment until you have all the details, but that you have all the details on the Treasury report right here. If nobody's interested in good news for Britain, you'll just go back to Downing Street and watch something on Netflix.

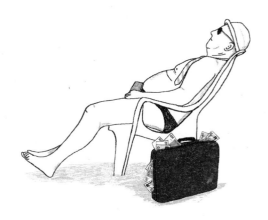

ANSWERS

How PM are you? (page 221)

Nobody said you had to stick to one answer for each decision, *did they*?

If you had the initiative to follow the following path to greatness, then get going! The nation needs your disarming, charismatic leadership.

Did you choose: **A4**, **B1** then **B4**, **C1**, **D5** then **D5** again, **E1** then **E4**, **F4**, **G4**, **H** all of them in order, **I3**, **J2**, **K1** for a laugh then **K4**, **L1** then **L4**?

If so, you're the perfect candidate to be modern, exciting prime minister. If you came within shouting distance of the correct route, you'll do. Congratulations, PRIME MINISTER!

If you ballsed it up a bit/lot, commiserations: you fucked that up, didn't you? That means you are entirely unsuitable for the top job. Which is a quality shared by almost every PM in living memory, so who knows anything in the end? Congratulations, PRIME MINISTER!

Yes/No (page 11)

1. **Y** – that's what politics means
2. **Y** – good: feel the power
3. **N** – staring without blinking makes you look hypnotised
4. **N** – under no circumstances, you will be humiliated
5. **N** – fuck them, this is YOUR moment

6. **N** – don't demean yourself, or make biscuit enemies
7. **N** – too many 'verys', you're not leading bloody North Korea
8. **Y** – good to have in your emotional back pocket

True or False? (page 26)

1. **100% false.**
2. **100% false.**
3. **100% true.**
4. **20% true only:** that was the name of his mistress.
5. **100% true.**
6. **20% true only:** she slept for that long, but not like that, obviously.
7. **100% false.**
8. **33% true:** he had a *four*-year affair with a Conservative minister.
9. **50% true:** he was a cousin of Rudyard Kipling. The 'Mr Kipling' name was just made up by the cake people.
10. **100% false**, in both directions.

How did you do? You need a minimum of six correct answers to be a plausible politics nerd. If you're a prospective prime minister, who gives a flying bollock – nobody's going to be testing you with rubbish like *this*, are they?

How's Your Day Looking? (page 38)

If you chose the following, you're absolutely ideal for the job, and for all the right reasons.

Scenario One: **fourth option.**
Scenario Two: **fourth option.**
Scenario Three: **first option.**
Scenario Four: **second option.**
Scenario Five: **first option.**

If you chose mostly third options, you might not last long as PM, but you would definitely leave your mark, and people would remember you for a very long time. Especially those you worked with, and their lawyers.

PM Pop Quiz (page 44)

1. C
2. B
3. D
4. C
5. A

CRISIS AT QUIZMAS (page 84)

If you answered mostly **A** *or* **B**:

You're probably thinking the more militant ends of the Conservative or Labour party might be a good fit. Or Reform. Or the Trade Union and Socialist Coalition. Well, the good news is that it doesn't actually matter that much. Half the art of politics is concealing what you really think, and saying things that resonate with voters. Your passion could lead you to the left or right and, let's be honest, there is something very relatable about a politician who can change their mind. Verdict: Tone it down a bit – go Labour or Conservative.

If you answered mostly **C**:

You need to carefully consider your career choices. You sound like a politician, which is bad news. Being measured and reasonable is a dead giveaway. Admittedly, this is what you'd sound like if you were prime minister, but you shouldn't be too boring and centrist before you start. Verdict: Retake the quiz, avoiding C. Pretend you're doing it for the first time, because after all, what is politics without pretence?

If you answered mostly **D**:

You should definitely think about starting your own party. Maybe think of yourself as a novelty parliamentary candidate to start with, spouting your mad, jokey crisis solutions from within a sexualised furry outfit or a full suit of armour. Once you've built a profile as your mad alter ego, you can announce that actually it's time the electorate saw the real you, and then wind your opinions back to normal. But only to a sort of normal. If voters are to come to terms with your real face and voice, there should still be a frisson of oddness, so maybe chuck in some impersonations or answer interview questions in iambic pentameter. Verdict: Go politically nuts, then less nuts.